C000053339

501 questions and answers for company directors and company secretaries

Roger Mason

THOROGOOD

Thorogood Publishing Ltd
10-12 Rivington Street
London EC2A 3DU
Telephone: 020 7749 4748
Fax: 020 7729 6110
Email: info@thorogood.ws
Web: www.thorogood.ws

A CIP catalogue record for this book is
available from the British Library.

RB: ISBN 1 85418 345 1
PB: ISBN 1 85418 340 0

Cover and book designed and typeset in
the UK by Driftdesign

Printed in India by Replika Press

The author

Roger Mason

Roger Mason is a highly experienced company director and company secretary. His early career was with Midland Bank and the Ford Motor Company before becoming finance director of ITC Entertainment Ltd. He was, for 14 years, company secretary and finance director of a leading British greetings card company. He lectures on finance and business matters and has written a number of books, including the best selling *Company Secretaries Desktop Guide, Credit Controllers Desktop Guide* and *The Complete Guide to Debt Recovery*.

Roger Mason presents seminars on the Essential Duties of a Company Director and the Essential Duties of a Company Secretary. Details can be obtained from:

UK Training (Worldwide) Ltd
4/5 The Mayflower
Liverpool Road
Formby
L37 6BU

Tel: 01704 878988
Website: www.uktrainingworldwide.com

Contents

two

Company constitution 37-92   **25**

three

Directors and Company Secretary 93-176   **53**

COMPANY SECRETARY
The position and the role   **86**

four

Rights and duties of Directors 177-212   **95**

five
Statutory registers and
Companies House 213-269   113

six

Shares, debentures and dividends 270-302   143

seven

Listed companies and corporate governance 303-324   **161**

eight

The elective regime, resolutions and notice 325-361   **173**

nine
Meetings 362-430   **193**

Good board meetings 217

MINUTES
General 219

ten
Accounts and audit 431-460

225

eleven
Financial difficulties, winding-up and striking off 461-501   **241**

Introduction

Introduction

This book has engendered a lot of interest in my family and friends. They have asked me many questions and it is very possible that some of my answers may be of interest. As the book follows a question and answer format I will answer the questions in this way.

What is the purpose of the book?

I want to give a lot of information in a way that will be readily understood. I have tried to choose questions that readers really would like answered, though of course you will have your own ideas on this.

Does the book cover everything that directors and company secretaries need to know?

No, that would obviously be impossible. The book concentrates very heavily on the Companies Act and associated matters and there is not space for the numerous other subjects with which directors and company secretaries must be involved. Even in these terms it cannot cover more than part. My copy of the Companies Act has 979 pages so even 501 questions will not deal with every topic.

Whose idea was the book?

It was mine but I am pleased to say that Thorogood did not need much persuading.

Why 501 questions?

Thorogood chose the number. It is a lot and it is intended to convey the impression that the book covers a great deal of material, which of course it does.

Was finding 501 questions a problem?

No. There could have been many more.

Was finding 501 answers a problem?

That took a little longer.

What was your biggest problem?

It was deciding in what order to put the questions. It was not easy to decide whether or not an explanation of the annual return should come before or after the rules for requisitioning an extraordinary general meeting. It was not like writing a crime novel where the body in the library is discovered near the beginning and Hercule Poirot unmasks the murderer in the last chapter.

Did you enjoy writing the book?

Yes.

I have followed my usual practice of using the masculine gender when referring to an anonymous single person such as a director. This avoids perpetually using 'he or she' or the grammatically nonsensical 'they'. Please believe that no disrespect is intended. Although the practice is losing ground, Parliament and Her Majesty's Government still frame and enact legislation in this way.

I have deliberately made a small number of questions similar to others in other parts of the book. I felt that this was necessary because they are relevant to more than one subject. For example the removal of auditors is relevant to the section on meetings and also the section on auditors.

Thank you for picking this particular book. I hope that you find it both interesting and useful.

Roger Mason

Important note concerning terms

The principal Act affecting company law, directors and company secretaries is the Companies Act 1985 as amended. In this book reference to 'the Act' means the Companies Act 1985, unless the context indicates otherwise.

The information in this book should be correct at the time of writing, however the law is complex and constantly changing. This book seeks to act as a guide through the maze but readers are advised to take legal advice where appropriate.

one

Company fundamentals 1-36

one
Company fundamentals

Basic questions

1   What is a company?

The term 'company' is commonly used meaning some association of people, as in a touring theatre company. The actors may or may not be associated with a registered company, and might be just a group of friends who enjoy putting on plays. It is a term frequently used by unincorporated sole traders and by partnerships. Thus 'Bill Smith and Company' could denote a sole trader or partnership, and not necessarily a registered company.

There have been companies incorporated by charters granted by the Crown and companies incorporated under the authority of Acts of Parliament. The South Seas Company of bubble fame was an example of the former, and the early railway companies were examples of the latter. Since 1844 Britain has had facilities for people to incorporate companies formed under the authority of the Companies Acts and register them with the Registrar of Companies. These are usually what people have in mind when they talk about companies. There are now almost two million such companies and they form an essential part of the life of the country, and in particular of its economic activity. The questions and answers in this book relate almost exclusively to companies registered under the Companies Acts.

2 What are the different types of company?

They are the following:

- Public company
- Private company limited by shares
- Private company limited by guarantee
- A company limited by guarantee and having a share capital
- Unlimited company

All public companies are limited by shares. All listed companies are public companies, although not all public companies are listed. All unlimited companies are private companies. Since 22nd December 1980 it has not been possible to register a new company limited by guarantee and having a share capital.

3 What are the differences between public companies and private companies?

Public companies must be limited by shares. They cannot be unlimited or limited by guarantee. Key differences include the following:

- The allotted value of the share capital of a public company must be at least £50,000, of which at least 25 per cent must be paid up. Any share premium must be 100 per cent paid up. There is no minimum sum for the share capital of a private company, although it cannot be NIL.
- Only a public company can be a listed company.
- Only a public company can issue a prospectus and offer its shares to the public.

More differences are detailed in the answer to the next question.

4   Are there any more differences between public companies and private companies?

Yes, there are. They include:

- The name of a public company must end with the words 'Public Limited Company', the abbreviation 'PLC' or the Welsh language equivalents.

- Public companies must have at least two members. Private companies can have a single member.

- Public companies must have at least two directors. If permitted by its articles (which Table A does not), a private company may have a sole director. A sole director cannot also be the company secretary.

5   What are the minimum and maximum possible amounts for a company's share capital?

There are no maximum amounts. The minimum amount for a public company is £50,000, of which at least 25 per cent (and 100 per cent of any share premium) must be paid up. There is no minimum amount for a private company, although it cannot be NIL. A number of private companies are registered with an authorised share capital of two shares of one penny each.

6   Can a company start trading (or operating) as soon as it has been registered?

A private company can start trading immediately. A public company may only do so when a certificate entitling it to commence trading has been issued by the Registrar. It should also be noted that it may not borrow until this certificate has been issued. Application for the certificate may be made on form 117. It is a statutory declaration that the value of the allotted share capital is at least £50,000, and it gives details of how the shares are paid up, preliminary expenses and any payments or benefits in favour of the promoter.

7 What exactly is meant when it is said that a company has a separate legal personality?

An incorporated company has a legal existence separate from the legal existence of its members. It can own property in its own name and it can sue and be sued in its own name. It can in some circumstances sue and be sued by its members. The principle that a company has a legal existence separate from that of its members was confirmed by the case *Salomon v Salomon and Co Ltd 1897*, one of the most celebrated cases in company law and possibly well known to you.

8 Exactly what does limited liability mean?

In the context of this question limited liability means the liability of the members, not of the directors or others. The overwhelming majority of companies are limited liability companies which means that the liability of the members is limited by shares or by guarantee. If a company is limited by shares, the liability of each member is limited to the full amount of the shares that he holds. Most shares are issued fully paid, so in the event of an insolvent liquidation the shares become worthless. If shares are partly paid, the members are liable to pay the uncalled part of their shares. If a company is limited by guarantee and it becomes insolvent, each member must contribute the amount of his guarantee.

9 Would you please give me some figures to show the expansion in the number of registered companies?

The concept of a private limited company dates back to 1907 and at that time there were less than 90,000 companies on the register. In recent years there has been an enormous increase in the number of companies on the active register. The figures (rounded to the nearest hundred) are:

	England and Wales	Scotland	Total
31st March 1995	926,500	55,300	981,800
31st March 2000	1,288,200	73,200	1,361,400
31st October 2004	1,816,700	103,300	1,920,000

Around 99.4 per cent of companies are private companies and only 0.6 per cent are public companies. Although Scotland has around ten per cent of the population it only has 5.4 per cent of the companies.

10   What are the alternatives to a company?

They include the following:

- Trading as a sole trader
- A general partnership
- A limited partnership
- A limited liability partnership (LLP)
- An unincorporated association
- A trust

Registration of companies

11   How is a company registered?

The following documents with the required fee must be submitted to the Registrar of Companies:

- A memorandum of association in the required form signed by the subscribers to the memorandum, and with each signature signed and attested by a witness.
- Articles of association signed and attested in the same way.
- Form 10 which gives details of the first directors and secretary with their consent to act, and the intended address of the registered office.
- Form 12 which is a statutory declaration of compliance. This must be signed by a director or secretary named on form 10, or by a solicitor engaged in the formation of the company.
- The formal approval of the name of the company (if required).

If everything is in order, the Registrar will issue a certificate of incorporation and place the company on the list of registered companies.

12   Is there a quick, cheap and easy way of getting my own company?

You should probably approach a company formation agent. These agents register and provide so called off-the-shelf companies. They register batches of companies with standard features and with them and their staff as the directors and secretary. The companies are kept dormant and have never traded. On application from you they will change the name (if required) and change the directors and secretary to people of your choice. Unless something out of the ordinary is wanted the whole thing should cost less than £100, plus the amount paid for the shares of course.

13   Is it possible to change a company's form of registration?

A company with a share capital cannot re-register as a company limited by guarantee, and a company limited by guarantee cannot re-register as a company with a share capital. Subject to complying with the correct procedures (which vary) the following is possible:

- A private company limited by shares can become a public company.

- An unlimited private company can become a public company.

- A public company can become a private company limited by shares or an unlimited private company.

- A private company limited by shares can become an unlimited private company.

- An unlimited private company can become a private company limited by shares.

14   Can a company registered in England and Wales change its place of registration to Scotland?

No, this is not possible, and neither can a company registered in Scotland change its place of registration to England and Wales. What you can do is register a new company in Scotland, then sell or transfer the first company's assets and business to it. Then the first company should be wound up or struck-off. Its name should then be available and the Scottish company should be able to change its name to that of the first company.

Companies limited by shares

15   What are the essential features of a company limited by shares?

The great majority of companies are limited by shares. They are either PLCs or private companies limited by shares. The obvious point to make is that in the event of the company becoming insolvent the liability of the members for the company's debts is limited by the amount of the shares that they hold. Their shares become worthless and they must pay up any unpaid sums on the shares, but that is the limit of their liability.

The fact that there are shares means that there is the prospect of the members receiving dividends. There is a lot of law about shares, share capital and dividends, and the provisions of the articles will be very relevant. Table A is the model set of articles for a public or private company that is limited by shares.

Unlimited companies

16   What are the essential features of an unlimited company?

The principal and obvious feature is that the members have unlimited, joint and severable liability for the company's debts. Another point is that the memorandum and articles must be in the form set out in Table E or as near as circumstances allow. Most unlimited companies are not required to file their accounts with the Registrar, though they must do so if the company is a holding company or subsidiary of a limited company.

17 What sort of organisation might suit being an unlimited company?

Given the potential liability such companies tend to be relatively small where the members can keep a close eye on them. They are sometimes used by professional practices as an alternative to partnerships.

18 Why would anyone in their right mind agree to be a member of an unlimited company?

Given the potential unlimited joint and severable liability your question is understandable, and there are only around 5,000 unlimited companies registered in Britain. One reason could be that the members want the world to know that they have total confidence in the company – it should impress the bank manager if the company asks for a loan. The members could be people who might be attracted to a general partnership, where the partners have unlimited liability, but want the structure of a company and company law.

Companies limited by guarantee

19 What are the essential features of a company limited by guarantee?

The members do not own shares with the consequence that dividends cannot be paid. Profits (or surpluses) are invested, retained in the company or spent in furtherance of the objects of the company. When the company is wound up the net assets are not paid to the members but distributed according to the objects and constitution of the company.

The members comprise the subscribers to the memorandum and such other persons as the directors approve for admission to membership. Each member signs a guarantee that in the event of the company becoming insolvent, he will contribute up to a specified sum. The amount of the guarantee is frequently nominal, such as, for example, ten members agreeing to contribute up to one pound each.

20 Are there minimum or maximum amounts for the guarantees in a company limited by guarantee?

No.

21 What sort of organisation might suit being a company limited by guarantee?

Companies limited by guarantee are often charitable organisations. They may appeal to sports associations, trade associations and flat management companies among others.

Community interest companies

22 What is a community interest company?

At the time of writing the Companies (Audit, Investigations and Community Enterprise) Bill is before Parliament. The Bill, which is likely to have become law before these words are read, provides for a new type of company to be known as a community interest company. Such companies will have to have 'Community Interest Company' or 'CIC' at the end of their names, so it could be, for example, 'Bognor Regis Affordable Childcare CIC Ltd'. It will be possible for a community interest company to be a PLC, a company limited by guarantee or a private company limited by shares. It is probable that most of them will be companies limited by guarantee.

23 Please tell me more about community interest companies?

The distinguishing features of a Community Interest Company will include the following:

1. It must show that it will pursue purposes beneficial to the community and not an unduly restricted group of beneficiaries.

2. Regulations may permit the exclusion of companies with certain objectives. Political parties and political campaigning organisations are probable examples.

3. A CIC will not be able to have charitable status. However, charities will be able to have CICs as subsidiaries.

4. A CIC will be required to produce an annual community interest company report. This will be publicly available at Companies House.

5. A CIC will be prohibited from distributing any profits to its members. However, a CIC that is limited by shares will have the option of issuing dividend-paying 'investor shares'. The dividends payable on such shares will be subject to a cap.

6. When a CIC is wound up its residual assets will not be distributed to its members, as in the case of a normal company. Instead, they will pass to another suitable organisation that has restrictions on the distribution of its profits, for example another CIC or a charity.

7. A regulator will be appointed to police and generally supervise CICs. The regulator will approve applications for CIC status and will have powers to investigate alleged abuses of CIC status. He will be able to remove directors, freeze assets and apply to the court for a CIC to be wound up.

8. A CIC will have none of the benefits or burdens of charitable status. It will not be subject to regulation by the Charity Commission or the charitable jurisdiction of the High Court.

24 What sort of companies might be community interest companies?

A Community Interest Company will be a non-profit distributing enterprise, but it will not be an option for a registered charity or a political party. It may, for example, be suitable for businesses operating in such areas as childcare, social housing, leisure and community transport. The special characteristics of the CIC are intended to make it a particularly suitable vehicle for some types of social enterprise – essentially, those that wish to work for community benefit within the relative freedom of the non-charitable company form, but with a clear assurance of non-profit-distribution status.

Shareholder agreements

25 Is it possible to have a shareholder agreement separate from the articles?

Yes, it is and it is quite common.

26 What is the point of shareholder agreements?

Shareholder agreements operate in addition to the articles of association. If well drafted, they bind the shareholders that are party to them, and this can be all of the shareholders. They may regulate the relationship of the shareholders and give rights and obligations that could not be put into the articles, or would not be appropriate for inclusion in the articles. For example, a shareholder agreement could give a minority shareholder the right to have a director of his choice on the board. It might be difficult or impossible to engineer this through the articles and there may not be the necessary level of support to change the articles. Shareholder agreements can be kept confidential, but this is not possible for the articles.

27 What sort of things might be suitable for inclusion in a shareholder agreement?

A minority shareholder in a private company can find himself effectively 'locked-in'. He may disagree with the direction that the company is taking but the majority decides and he could be perpetually outvoted. It may be difficult or impossible to sell his shares because any buyer would face the same problems. A shareholder agreement might overcome this difficulty by providing a basis for the valuation of the shares, and by providing an opportunity or compulsion for the other shareholders to buy them. It can also give the other shareholders first refusal.

There are many other possibilities. They include the right to be a director or have a nominated person as a director and the right to act as a consultant. They can include such things as the obligations of the shareholders to provide loan finance if it is needed.

Company seal

28 What is the company seal?

The company seal (or common seal) may be likened to the corporate signature of the company. It is normally a small hand-held device for making an impression on paper or wax, though occasionally a splendid, large contraption may be encountered. It is a specific requirement that the company's registered name be incorporated into the design of the company seal.

The company seal is required for deeds, contracts without consideration, share certificates and certain other documents. It may be used on documents where there is no legal requirement that the seal be used.

29 Is it compulsory for a company to have a company seal?

No, it is not compulsory, though it was until 30th July 1990. However, many companies choose to still have and use a company seal even though it is no longer a requirement. Section 36(A)(4) of the Act states:

'A document signed by a director and the secretary of a company, or by two directors of a company, and expressed (in whatever form of words) to be executed by the company has the same effect as if executed under the common seal of the company.'

There are now three possibilities:

- A company can have a company seal and use it.

- A company can decide not to have a company seal and use a suitable form of words instead.

- A company can have a company seal but, on some or all occasions when its use would be required, elect to use a suitable form of words instead.

30   What is a suitable form of words when the company seal is not used?

If a document is intended to be a deed, and whose wording makes that fact clear, it will upon delivery have the effect of a deed. An example of such wording is:

Executed by ....………………….. Ltd as a deed and signed by

……………………................:... Director

……………………................... Company Secretary

Alternatively the signatories may be two directors.

31   What records should be kept of the use of the company seal?

The use of the company seal should be approved by the directors, or a committee of the directors, and this should be evidenced by a retrospective board minute that identifies the document on which the seal was used. If the company seal is used a lot, it is not desirable to have a string of individual board minutes. Instead, all the uses should be entered in a Sealings Register. Blocks of entries in the register can then, from time to time, be approved by the directors and these decisions should be minuted.

The requirements concerning directors' approval, minutes and a sealing register are exactly the same if a form of words is used instead of the company seal.

32   Are the articles relevant?

They may be. Regulation 101 of Table A states:

> 'The seal shall only be used by the authority of the directors or of a committee of directors authorised by the directors. The directors may determine who shall sign any instrument to which the seal is affixed and unless otherwise so determined it shall be signed by a director and by the secretary or by a second director.'

Officers of the company

33 Who is an officer of the company?

Section 744 of the Act defines 'officer' as:

'in relation to a body corporate, includes a director, manager or secretary.'

This is not a very satisfactory definition because the term 'manager' is not defined, and the word 'includes' poses the obvious question of who else might be considered an officer. The next Companies Act may well provide a better definition.

All directors (including non-executive directors) are always officers, and so are all company secretaries. A company's auditor is an officer for just some purposes. The position of managers varies according to circumstances. If there is an active board of directors running the company on a day to day basis, the managers would probably not be held to be officers. On the other hand, if the board is totally non-executive, a general manager with day to day control would almost certainly be an officer.

34 What are the consequences of being an officer of the company?

The Act is peppered with many references to the term 'officer', and it gives them certain rights and many responsibilities. Various other Acts also give responsibilities to officers. The officers of a company are accountable for it and what it does. The Companies Act provides more than 200 offences that can be committed by officers. Just one example is section 288 which relates to the register of directors and secretaries and relevant notifications to Companies House. Subsection 4 states:

'If an inspection required under this section is refused, or if default is made in complying with subsection (1) or (2), the company and every officer of it who is in default is liable to a fine and, for continued contravention, to a daily default fine.'

Just one example from another Act is section 212 of the Insolvency Act which relates to the penalisation of directors and officers. It specifically relates to (among others) *'a person who is or has been an officer of the company'*.

On a different tack, a company's financial statements must disclose certain transactions with its officers.

35   Can all officers commit all the offences?

No, some offences can only be committed by the directors. For example, the directors are required to prepare proper accounts, formally approve them and one director must sign the balance sheet. Only a director can sign the balance sheet and only the directors commit an offence if it is not done.

36   I am an officer of the company and it all sounds rather worrying. How worried should I be?

You should certainly take your responsibilities seriously but perhaps you should not worry too much. The great majority of officers manage without too many problems. You might take comfort from the fact that a fine or penalty can only be imposed if the officer acted 'knowingly and wilfully'. Section 730(5) of the Act states:

> *'For the purpose of any enactment in the Companies Acts which provides that an officer of a company (or other body) who is in default is liable to a fine or penalty, the expression "officer who is in default" means any officer of the company (or other body) who knowingly and wilfully authorises or permits the default, refusal or contravention mentioned in the enactment.'*

two

Company constitution 37-92

two
Company constitution

MEMORANDUM OF ASSOCIATION

Basic questions

37   Just what is the memorandum?

The constitution of a company is contained in its memorandum and articles of association and they may be likened to a contract between the members. The first memorandum must be signed by the subscribers to the memorandum (the founder members) and delivered to the Registrar of Companies as part of the company formation process. It is binding on the members and, subject to conditions, may be amended by them later. The memorandum must contain prescribed information and it governs the company's relationship with the outside world.

38   What are the requirements concerning the form and layout of the memorandum?

The memorandum must be in the relevant statutory form or as near to it as circumstances permit. The relevant forms are set out in the Companies (Tables A to F) Regulations 1985 (SI 1985/805). The tables are:

Table B   A private company limited by shares

Table C   A company limited by guarantee not having a share capital

Table D A public company limited by guarantee and having a share capital and a private company limited by guarantee and having a share capital

Table E An unlimited company having a share capital

Table F A public company limited by shares

In practice the memorandum is almost always printed but this is not a legal requirement.

39 What must be included in the memorandum of a company limited by shares?

The following must be included:

1. the name of the company;

2. if it is to be a public company, that fact;

3. the situation of the registered office, i.e. whether it is in England and Wales, or Wales, or Scotland;

4. the objects of the company;

5. if relevant, that the liability of the members is limited; and

6. the amount of authorised share capital and its division into shares of a fixed amount. The share capital may be denominated in any currency and different currencies may be used for different classes, except that a public company must have its minimum capital denominated in sterling. If an unlimited company has a share capital, this must be stated in the articles, not in the memorandum.

The memorandum ends with a formal subscription clause.

40 What must be included in the memorandum of a company limited by guarantee?

The following must be included:

1. the name of the company;

2. the situation of the registered office, i.e. whether it is in England and Wales, or Wales, or Scotland;

3.   the objects of the company;

4.   a statement that the liability of the members is limited; and

5.   the amount of the guarantee, i.e. the maximum amount that each member undertakes to contribute in the event of a winding up.

Other clauses are often included. They may, for example, include provisions prohibiting the distribution of profits and specifying the application of assets on winding up.

The memorandum ends with a formal subscription clause.

41   What are the consequences of stating that the company is a public limited company?

The name of the company must end in 'Public Limited Company' or 'p.l.c.'.

The company will be a public company for all purposes and all the consequences will apply. The consequences are not listed in a single, easily-accessible place, but they include the following:

- Only a public company can issue a prospectus and offer shares to the public.

- A public company must have at least two directors. If permitted by its articles, a private company can have a sole director.

- There are extra requirements concerning the qualifications of the company secretary.

42   Who has the right to see the memorandum?

The memorandum is available to anyone at all at Companies House. A company is required to send to any member, on request, an up to date copy of the memorandum and articles. It must incorporate any alterations that have been made, and must include copies of any resolutions of the company which were required to be filed at the Companies Registry. A charge not exceeding 5p may be made, though almost all companies would waive this trivial sum.

Changes to the memorandum

43 May the memorandum be changed after incorporation and, if so, how is it done?

- The country of incorporation (England and Wales or Scotland) cannot be altered.

- The amount of the authorised share capital may be increased by an ordinary resolution of the members.

- A company limited by guarantee may not alter the clause that sets out the guarantee.

- The company name, the objects clause, and any condition (other than a provision which confers rights upon a particular class of member) which could lawfully have been contained in the articles may be altered by a special resolution of the members.

- A certified copy of any resolution to alter the memorandum must be delivered to Companies House within 15 days of it being passed.

- Additional procedures are required for certain changes, an example being the change from an unlimited company to a limited company.

44 May certain parts of the memorandum be entrenched so that they cannot be altered?

Yes! A company's constitution may specify that a majority higher than the 75 per cent normally needed for a special resolution be required to change some or all parts of the memorandum. If such a higher majority is obtained, it still counts as a special resolution. Any provision calling for less than 75 per cent is inoperative and 75 per cent will still be needed. It is possible to specify that 100 per cent support is required to make a particular change or any change. The provision requiring more than 75 per cent support can itself normally be changed provided that the required level of support to change it is obtained. However, this can be made impossible by phrasing a relevant clause 'no alteration may be made to clause... or to this clause'.

It may be possible to entrench some or all parts of the memorandum by a suitably worded shareholders agreement. This will be a contract and not part of the memorandum.

45 Are there any provisions for a dissatisfied member to object to a change in the memorandum that has been agreed by the required resolution of the members?

Yes, but only in respect of an alteration to the objects. An application may be made to the Court for the alteration to be cancelled. The application must be made within 21 days of the passing of the resolution and may be made by:

1. the holders of 15 per cent in nominal value of the company's share capital or any class thereof; or

2. if the company is not limited by shares, 15 per cent of its members; or

3. the holders of 15 per cent of debentures secured by a floating charge and issued before 1 December 1947.

The court may confirm the alteration, confirm it with conditions or cancel it.

Company name

46 What are the requirements that the company name should correctly designate the type of company?

If the company is a public company, the name must end with 'Public Limited Company' or 'p.l.c.'.

If the company is a private limited company, the name must end with 'Limited' or 'Ltd'.

When community interest companies are possible and if it is such a company, the indication of the type of company must be preceded by one of:

- Community Interest Public Limited Company

- Community Interest PLC

- Community Interest Company

- CIC

These designations must appear at the end of the name, not in any other position. The Welsh language equivalents may be used if the company's registered office is in Wales.

47 Are there any exceptions to the requirement for a private company to include 'Limited' or 'Ltd' in its name?

It is sometimes felt that the use of 'Limited' or 'Ltd' is undesirable when a company has charitable or philanthropic objects. In particular, it is sometimes felt that people might wrongly assume that such a company has profit-making objectives. Section 30(3) of the Act specifies that 'Limited' or 'Ltd' may be omitted from the name of a company limited by guarantee provided that:

'a) the objects of the company are (or in the case of a company about to be registered, are to be) the promotion of commerce, art, science, education, religion, charity or any profession, and anything incidental or conducive to any of those objects; and

b) the company's memorandum or articles of association:

i) require its profits (if any) or other income to be applied in promoting its objects;

ii) prohibit the payment of dividends to its members, and

iii) require all the assets which would otherwise be available to its members generally to be transferred on its winding up either to another body with objects similar to its own or to another body the objects of which are the promotion of charity and anything incidental or conducive thereto (whether or not the body is a member of the company).'

Different requirements applied to companies registered before the Companies Act 1981 came into force.

48   What stops a company having a name that is the same as, or similar to, the name of another company?

The Registrar will refuse to register a name that is identical to a name that is already registered and for this purpose the designation at the end of the name is disregarded. So Bognor Regis Software Limited may not be registered if Bognor Regis Software p.l.c. is already on the register. The Registrar will register a name that is similar to (but not identical to) the name of a company that is already registered. However, the second company may subsequently be ordered to change its name.

49   Are there any other limitations on the choice of name?

Yes, there are and they may be summarised as follows:

1. A name may not be registered if in the opinion of the Secretary of State (in practice the Registrar of Companies) it is offensive or its use would constitute a criminal offence.

2. A name may only be registered with the permission of the Secretary of State if it implies that the company is connected with central or local government.

3. There is a list of words and expressions that may only be used with the permission of the Secretary of State. 'University' is an example of such a word. The words and expressions are listed in SIs 1981/1685, 1982/1653, 1992/1196 and 1995/3022.

50   Can a company be ordered to change its name?

Yes, it can. The Secretary of State (in practice the Registrar of Companies) can order a company to change its name. She may do this if, in her opinion, the name is 'too like' a name that was already registered or should have been already registered at the time that it was registered. She may do this within 12 months of registration.

51 Are there any other circumstances in which a company may be ordered to change its name?

Yes, there are and they may be summarised as follows:

1. A company has supplied misleading information.

2. A company has given undertakings or assurances that it has not fulfilled.

3. The name of the company (in the opinion of the Secretary of State) gives so misleading an indication of the nature of its activities that harm is likely to be caused to the public.

There is a time limit of five years for points 1 and 2, but no time limit for point 3.

52 Can I ask the Registrar of Companies to order a company to change its name?

Yes, you can. You should write to the Registrar of Companies giving your reasons, with as much supporting evidence as you can. They could, for example, include evidence of misdirected post, misleading advertisements, letters from confused customers, etc. Remember that circumstances alter cases. A nationally known company, such as Marks and Spencer p.l.c., may find it easier to show that people are confused. It may be much more difficult for a small company if the object of the complaint is another small company, with different suppliers, different customers, different products and which operates in a different part of the country.

53 How can I easily check all the requirements concerning company names?

Companies House publishes, free of charge, a very helpful guidance booklet, GBF2.

Place of registration and the registered office

54   What are the options for the location of the registered office?

The options are:

- England and Wales

- Wales

- Scotland

Approximately 94 per cent of companies are registered in England and Wales, and approximately 6 per cent of companies are registered in Scotland. The number of companies registered in Wales is very small and well under 1 per cent of the total. Companies registered in Northern Ireland, Isle of Man, Jersey, Guernsey or any other country or territory are not within the scope of this book.

55   What are the consequences of the location of the registered office?

If it is located in England and Wales or Wales, the company will be registered at Companies House in Cardiff. If it is located in Scotland, it will be registered at Companies House in Edinburgh. The place of registration cannot be changed and the company must always submit the annual return, accounts, company forms, etc to either Cardiff or Edinburgh according to the original decision.

The statutory registers and certain other documents must always be kept in the country of incorporation (England and Wales, Wales or Scotland), though not necessarily at the registered office.

If the registered office is located in England and Wales or Wales, English law will apply. If it is in Scotland, Scottish law will apply. Company law is in most cases the same but it is administered by English judges and Scottish judges. This has resulted in a few differences of interpretation.

56 Are there any more consequences of the location of the registered office?

Yes, there are three, as follows:

1. The Registrar of Companies will communicate with the company at its registered office. Communications may, for example, include reminders concerning late receipt of annual returns or annual accounts.

2. Anyone can communicate with the company at its registered office. For example, a legal document is validly served if it is delivered to the registered office. This is true even if the company has gone away from its registered office. It is the responsibility of the directors to change the registered office if necessary, and they must bear the consequences of not doing so.

3. Allocation of a company to a tax district is a matter for the Inland Revenue. However, a change in the address of its registered office may well result in the company being transferred to a different tax district. This may sometimes be wanted if relations with a particular tax district are not good, though of course the Inland Revenue would probably contend that the standard of all tax districts is broadly similar and broadly satisfactory. If the address of the registered office is changed for this purpose, it may be necessary to move it a certain distance. Next door will probably not achieve the desired result.

57 Can a PO Box Number be used as the registered office?

No, it cannot. The registered office must be a physical place that can be visited.

58 Must the registered office be an actual office of the company?

No, it is not a requirement and many companies do use other locations. Frequent choices are the company's solicitors, accountants or company secretary, if not an employee. Any address will do.

If the registered office is not an office of the company, it is important that arrangements are made for the speedy forwarding of post and other documents. Certain time limits may start running from the delivery of documents to the registered office, whether or not they have actually been received by company officers or staff.

59   How is the address of the registered office changed?

The registered office may only be moved within the territory of incorporation. This means, for example, that it may be moved from London to Birmingham, but not from London to Glasgow. The decision to change the address of the registered office is made by the directors, not the members.

Notice of the change must be given to the Registrar on form 287 and it is not effective until the change has been registered by the Registrar. During a period of 14 days after registration by the Registrar any document may be validly served at either the old or the new registered offices. It will be necessary to alter company notepaper to show the new address.

60   What are the consequences if the memorandum stipulates that the registered office will be in Wales?

They are as follows:

1.   The name of the company may (but not must) end in 'cyfyngedig' instead of 'limited' or 'cwmni cyfyngedig cyhoeddus' instead of 'public limited company'. The permitted abbreviations are 'cyf' and 'ccc' respectively.

2.   The company may (but not must) register its memorandum and articles in Welsh. If it does so, Companies House will provide an English language translation and both will be put on the public record.

3.   Other documents and returns may (but not must) be provided to the registrar in Welsh. Some of them (but only some of them) must be accompanied by a certified English language translation.

Objects clause

61 What is the purpose of the objects clause?

Directors are trusted by the members to run their company for them. Furthermore, they are trusted by the members to do their best to safeguard their investment in the company. This is usually in the form of share capital but the members may be at risk because of guarantees. In an unlimited company the risk to the members is unlimited. It is a very big responsibility and the objects clause limits the directors to pursuing objects for which the members have given their permission. If you gave someone some money to do things with for your benefit, you would probably want to know what he was going to do with it.

62 I have noticed that many objects clauses seem very long. Why is this?

You are very observant and you are quite correct. Objects clauses sometimes cover several pages and list the objects in tedious detail. They often contain many expressions such as 'all powers incidental to'. In fact the directors may be able to do almost anything.

This may be because of a wish for precise definition and it may be because of a wish to allow directors to do everything that they want to do in running the company. It may be an attempt to ensure that the directors are not caught out. In that case you might think that the practice negates the purpose of the objects clause, and you would not be alone in holding this opinion. Of course a long and wide objects clause is only in place at the wish of the members. They do not have to agree.

63 I have heard that some companies have the object 'to carry on the business of a general commercial company'. What exactly does this mean?

This gives the directors the power to do all things as are incidental or conducive to the carrying on of any trade or business. It can be a stand-alone object or buttressed with others, and is adequate in many circumstances. Of course, it should only be adopted if the members wish to give the directors this very wide discretion. This provision is only relevant to commercial companies. It is not, for example, relevant to a company that is a charity.

64   What are the possible consequences if the directors pursue objects not permitted by the objects clause?

The directors are acting *ultra vires* (beyond their powers) and are liable to compensate the members for the consequences of so doing. Of course if there are no harmful consequences the issue does not arise. However, the consequences can be serious for the directors. Permission for an *ultra vires* act by the directors may be given by the members by means of a special resolution with a 75 per cent majority. This is best done in advance but such an act may be ratified retrospectively. An *ultra vires* act is binding on the company as regards third parties. It is a problem between the directors and the members.

65   What is the future of the objects clause?

The Company Law Review Steering Group recommended that the concept of a compulsory objects clause should be abolished. This would leave directors free to act as they wished, so long as they were genuinely trying to serve the interests of the company and its members. It is likely that the next Companies Act will incorporate this proposal. If and when this does happen, it will still be open to members to insert an objects clause into the constitution if they wish, but it probably will not be done in most companies.

Authorised share capital and the guarantee

66   What is meant by the term 'authorised share capital'?

The authorised share capital is the total value of the shares that the company can issue, as opposed to the issued share capital which is the shares that the company has issued. Obviously the issued share capital must not be greater than the authorised share capital. The authorised share capital is sometimes set at a very large figure in order to make it easier to issue new shares later if desired. The memorandum must specify the total authorised amount and how it is divided into shares. A typical clause is:

'The company's share capital is £1,000,000 divided into 1,000,000 shares of £1 each.'

Any division into classes of shares can be specified in the memorandum but there are advantages in doing it in the articles.

67   What does the Companies Act say about the guarantee?

The guarantee is only applicable to a company limited by guarantee. Section 2(4) of the Act puts it as follows:

'The memorandum of a company limited by guarantee must also state that each member undertakes to contribute to the assets of the company if it should be wound up while he is a member, or within one year after he ceases to be a member, for payment of the debts and liabilities of the company contracted before he ceases to be a member, and of the costs, charges and expenses of winding up, and for adjustment of the rights of the contributories among themselves, such amount as may be required, not exceeding a specified amount.'

Subscription clause

68   What goes into the subscription clause?

The subscription clause is as set out in the appropriate table. The following is taken from Table B for a private company limited by shares.

We, the subscribers to this memorandum of association, wish to be formed into a company pursuant to this memorandum; and we agree to take the number of shares shown opposite our respective names.

Names and Addresses of Subscribers	Number of shares taken by each Subscriber
1. Thomas Jones, 138 Mountfield Street, Tredegar.	1
2. Mary Evans, 19 Merthyr Road, Aberystwyth.	1
	2

Dated _____

Witness to the above signatures _____

Anne Brown, "Woodlands", Fieldside Road, Bryn Mawr.

Disclosure of statutory information

69   Why is it necessary to disclose and publicise certain statutory information?

Owning a company is a privilege, and owning a limited liability company is a very considerable privilege. It is felt right that in return certain statutory information should be drawn to the attention of people who have dealings with the company. The short answer to the question is that it is a legal requirement.

A further very practical reason should be mentioned. It is dangerous not to disclose that a company is a limited company if this is the case. This is because people might reasonably assume that they are dealing with a sole trader or partnership operating without limited liability. If there has not been proper disclosure, in the event of insolvency one or more people might find themselves personally responsible for certain company debts.

70 What is the requirement to display the company name outside its business premises?

Section 348(1) of the Act states:

> *'Every company shall paint or affix, and keep painted or affixed, its name on the outside of every office or place in which its business is carried on, in a conspicuous position and in letters easily legible.'*

This is slightly ambiguous in one or two ways, including the position when the company occupies a small part of a large office block. It is generally considered acceptable for the name to be displayed outside the first relevant internal door leading to the company's premises.

It is generally considered prudent that the name be displayed outside the registered office, even if the company does not carry on business at it. You may have seen large numbers of company names displayed outside the offices of firms of solicitors and accountants. This is because their offices are the registered offices of many companies. The name that must be displayed is the name that appears in the memorandum. A trade name is not sufficient.

71 What information must be given on company business letters and order forms?

The following information must be shown. It is usual to group all the information in small print at the bottom of the page but the location is not a legal requirement.

1. The full registered name of the company.

2. The place of registration. This may be shown as:
    *   England
    *   England and Wales
    *   Wales

- Scotland

- Cardiff

- Edinburgh

3.   The company's registered number.

4.   The address of the registered office and the fact that it is the registered office.

If a company is permitted to not use the word 'Limited' or the abbreviation 'Ltd' in its name, the fact that it is a limited company must be disclosed. If a company is a charity and does not have the words 'charity' or 'charitable' in its name, the fact that it is a charity must be disclosed.

72   With reference to the last question – what exactly is meant by 'order form'?

It is ambiguous because it could be taken to mean purchase orders placed by the company or forms which the company makes available for other persons to order goods and services from the company. In the view of the DTI it means forms which the company makes available for other persons to order goods and services from the company.

73   Are there other requirements concerning the disclosure of information on business letters?

Yes, there are a few:

1.   If the name or nationality of any director is stated, the names or nationalities of all the directors must be stated. A name written or typed as part of a letter or placed under a signature does not trigger this requirement.

2.   If any reference is made to the amount of the share capital, which is not obligatory and is not usual, the reference must be to paid-up share capital.

3.   If the company is an investment company within the meaning of section 266 of the Act, the fact that it is such a company must be disclosed.

74 Must the company's registered name be given in other documents?

Section 349(1) of the Act states:

'Every company shall have its name mentioned in characters:

a) in all business letters of the company,

b) in all its notices and other official publications,

c) in all bills of exchange, promissory notes, endorsements, cheques and orders for money or goods purporting to be signed by or on behalf of the company, and

d) in all its bills of parcels, invoices, receipts and letters of credit.'

The name of the company must also be given on the company seal if there is one.

75 Is there a requirement to show the statutory information on company business e-mails?

It is not free from all doubt, but it is generally thought that there is no such requirement. This is because e-mails were not known when the law was enacted. It is expected that it will be made a requirement by the next main Companies Act.

76 I have noted that quite a few companies seem not to fully comply. Am I right and does it matter?

You are very observant and you are quite right. Quite a few companies do not get it exactly right, often on a technicality. Fortunately for them the law is not often vigorously enforced in this area. An easy mistake to make is to assume that putting just one address (which is the registered office as well as a trading address) at the top of the notepaper is proper disclosure of the registered office. It is necessary to put 'registered office' in brackets or put something like 'registered office as above'.

It should matter because a mistake is an offence and bad for the company's image. There is also the factor that some mistakes can leave one or more persons personally liable for company debts.

ARTICLES OF ASSOCIATION

Basic questions

77   What are the articles of association?

The articles of association govern the way in which a company's internal affairs are regulated. They may be likened to an agreement between the members and binding on them. Articles registered at the time of incorporation must, if the company is registered by the submission of paper documents, be signed by the subscribers and the signatures must be attested by witnesses.

78   Are the articles of association important? Why are there not more questions about them in this section of the book?

The articles of association are extremely important. This section of the book covers the general principles. However, answers to questions on very many topics are likely to include phrases such as 'subject to the articles' and 'you should refer to the articles to answer this question'. The issues are addressed topic by topic throughout the book rather than all in one place. To repeat the point – yes, the articles of association are important.

79   How much freedom do the members have concerning the articles?

They have a lot of freedom, though they cannot override the Companies Act and they cannot commit a fraud on the minority. The members own the company and so, within limits, they can have what rules they want. No one is forced to be a member of a company.

80   Are there any requirements concerning format and presentation?

The articles of association must be printed and divided into consecutively numbered paragraphs. The word 'printing' permits, for example, a good quality photocopy of a typed document.

81 I have heard of model sets of articles in the form of tables. What does this mean?

For companies registered on or after 1st July 1985 you are referring to the Companies (Tables A to F) Regulations 1985, SI 1985/805 as amended by SI 1985/1052 and 2000/3373 in relation to electronic communications between companies and their members. These are model sets of articles for the different types of company as follows:

Table A A company limited by shares

Table C A company limited by guarantee and not having a share capital

Table D A company (public or private) limited by guarantee and having a share capital

Table E An unlimited company having a share capital

Table A relates to more than 95 per cent of all companies and Table C relates to the majority of the remainder. Different Tables (still called Table A etc) relate to companies registered under the different Companies Acts and registered before 1st July 1985.

The tables are model sets of articles available for adoption but they are not compulsory.

82 My company was registered before 1st July 1985. What difference does it make and does it matter?

Your company is regulated by one of the earlier tables. This could be 1948, 1929 or even earlier. If you have special articles it may be less significant, but one of the earlier tables will be your default provision. This might not matter too much because in many ways the tables have remained similar. However, there are differences so you should not just assume that you can check something off in the latest table. It could matter because some people might not appreciate the potential problem.

It is not difficult to update your articles to the latest table or to make the latest table your default provision, provided that the members are willing to do so of course. You just need a short special resolution of the members.

You might like to double check that this has not been done at some time in the past.

83   I notice that Table C is much shorter than Table A. Does this mean that it is easier to use and that there are fewer regulations governing a company limited by guarantee?

Your observation is correct. Table A contains 118 regulations whereas Table C contains just 13, but neither of the conclusions are justified. This is because Table C states that most of Table A will apply, but that some of the regulations are excluded. Thirteen additional ones are then listed. If your company is limited by guarantee you will need to refer to both Table C and Table A.

84   What are the basic choices concerning articles?

There are three possibilities:

1. The relevant table (almost always Table A or Table C) can be adopted in its entirety and without modification.

2. The relevant table can be rejected and specially written articles adopted instead.

3. The relevant table can be adopted but modified to suit a company's particular needs. If this is done, the articles will normally start with a phrase such as 'The company shall adopt Table A save as follows'. The articles will then go on to exclude certain regulations from Table A and list specially written regulations.

A company limited by shares may be registered with its memorandum endorsed 'Registered without articles of association'. If this is done, Table A in its entirety will apply. Other types of company are not permitted to do this and must register articles, though a simple reference to the relevant table is sufficient.

If you are forming a company and not adopting the relevant table, you could write the articles yourself but this would probably not be a good idea. It would probably be necessary to get legal advice. Various trade associations and similar bodies provide specimen sets of articles for the use of their members. Also certain legal stationers provide them. There are a lot of possibilities. Specially written articles often include many of the regulations from Table A or Table C.

85 What issues are covered by the articles?

The possibilities are extensive but the following subject headings are included in Table A.

Interpretation	Regulation 1
Share Capital	Regulations 2 – 5
Share Certificates	Regulations 6 – 7
Lien	Regulations 8 – 11
Calls on Shares And Forfeiture	Regulations 12 – 22
Transfer Of Shares	Regulations 23 – 28
Transmission Of Shares	Regulations 29 – 31
Alteration Of Share Capital	Regulations 32 – 34
Purchase Of Own Shares	Regulation 35
General Meetings	Regulations 36 – 37
Notice Of General Meetings	Regulations 38 – 39
Proceedings At General Meetings	Regulations 40 – 53
Votes Of Members	Regulations 54 – 63
Number Of Directors	Regulation 64
Alternate Directors	Regulations 65 – 69
Powers Of Directors	Regulations 70 – 71
Delegation Of Directors' Powers	Regulation 72
Appointment And Retirement of Directors	Regulations 73 – 80
Disqualification And Removal Of Directors	Regulation 81
Remuneration Of Directors	Regulation 82
Directors' Expenses	Regulation 83

Directors' Appointments And Interests   Regulations 84 – 86

Directors' Gratuities And Pensions   Regulation 87

Proceedings Of Directors   Regulations 88 – 98

Secretary   Regulation 99

Minutes   Regulation 100

The Seal   Regulation 101

Dividends   Regulations 102 – 108

Accounts   Regulation 109

Capitalisation Of Profits   Regulation 110

Notices   Regulations 111 – 116

Winding-Up   Regulation 117

Indemnity   Regulation 118

86   What does the term 'default provision' mean in relation to articles?

It means that each of the regulations in the relevant table will automatically apply to a company unless it has registered articles that exclude them. For example, Regulation 40 of Table A states *'Two persons entitled to vote upon the business to be transacted, each being a member or a proxy for a member or a duly authorised representative of a corporation, shall be a quorum.'* This is not compulsory and members are free to fix any other number, including just one person. However, if articles do not specify a number for a quorum or are not inconsistent with Table A, then Regulation 40 of Table A will apply.

87   Can the articles override the provisions of the Companies Act or other Acts?

No, they cannot. For example, a change to the company's name requires a special resolution passed with a 75 per cent majority. If the articles state that a two thirds majority is sufficient, the Act will prevail and a 75 per cent majority will still be required.

88 Does Table A allow the directors as a whole to terminate the appointment of a director?

No, it does not. If Table A applies and if a director is not disqualified in some way and will not resign, he may only be removed by a vote of the members. Special articles often do give the directors the power to terminate the appointment of a director. Listed companies invariably provide for this and many other companies do too.

89 What does Table A say about directors retiring by rotation?

Regulation 73 provides:

> 'At the first annual general meeting all the directors shall retire from office, and at every subsequent annual general meeting one-third of the directors who are subject to retirement by rotation or, if their number is not three or a multiple of three, the number nearest to one-third shall retire from office; but, if there is only one director who is subject to retirement by rotation, he shall retire.'

Special articles may change this and many variations are found. Sometimes every director retires at every annual general meeting. Sometimes directors do not retire at all and serve until they die, resign, become disqualified in some way or are removed.

90 Does Table A allow for a sole director?

No, it does not. Regulation 64 provides:

> 'Unless otherwise determined by ordinary resolution, the number of directors (other than alternate directors) shall not be subject to any maximum but shall not be less than two.'

Special articles in a private company can provide for a sole director and it is not uncommon. The Act requires that a public company has a minimum of two directors.

Changes to the articles

91   Can the articles be changed and if so how is it done?

Yes, the articles may be changed. It requires a special resolution of the members passed with a 75 per cent majority. A certified copy of the reso-lution must be delivered to the Registrar of Companies within 15 days of it being passed. This must be accompanied by a printed set of the articles as altered. If the alteration is minor and easy to follow, an altered copy of the articles will suffice.

92   I act for a company limited by guarantee that is a registered charity. Are there any special requirements relating to an alteration to the articles?

Yes, there are if the alteration 'is a provision directing or restricting the manner in which the property of the company may be used or applied'. In this case the prior written consent of the Charity Commissioners must be obtained and this must be lodged with the copy of the special resolution delivered to the Registrar of Companies.

three

Directors and Company Secretary 93-176

three

Directors and Company Secretary

DIRECTORS

Basic questions

93 What is meant by the terms executive director and non-executive director, and what are the differences?

All directors attend board meetings and vote, and are responsible for the general running of the company, setting policies, stewardship of company assets, compliance with the law and good practice, etc and share overall responsibility for matters that are within the sphere of directors' duties.

An executive director may well be a full-time director, though this is not necessarily the case. He will do a day to day executive job. A typical example might be a sales director who leads and directs the sales force and sales effort, and may personally sell to customers. It may not be literally true, but you will probably understand what is meant if it is said that an executive director gets his hands dirty.

A non-executive director, on the other hand, does not do a day to day executive job in the company. He 'just' has all the responsibilities mentioned in the first paragraph of this answer. A non-executive chairman has responsibility for running the board but a non-executive sales director is a contradiction in terms.

94 That's all very well but can you please give more details about the role of non-executive directors?

Certainly, but the first paragraph in the last answer seems quite comprehensive. It refers to all directors and this term, of course, embraces the non-executive directors. Perhaps it is worth repeating.

All directors attend board meetings and vote, and are responsible for the general running of the company, setting policies, stewardship of company assets, compliance with the law and good practice, etc and share overall responsibility for matters that are within the sphere of directors' duties.

Non-executive directors are frequently well-connected and bring to the company a wide range of contacts and experience. The Combined Code emphasises the distinction between independent non-executive directors and those who cannot be classed as independent. The latter category includes, for example, a former managing director of the company.

Non-executive directors frequently serve on audit committees and other committees, and their detachment makes them particularly suitable for this. The Combined Code includes the following:

'The board should establish an audit committee of at least three, or in the case of smaller companies two, members, who should all be independent non-executive directors. The board should satisfy itself that at least one member of the audit committee has recent and relevant financial experience.'

The Combined Code also calls for independent non-executive directors to constitute a remuneration committee. Non-executive directors may have a particularly important role in liasing with shareholders and particularly with institutional shareholders.

95 What is meant by the term 'unified board' and do we have them in Britain?

It is tempting to be facetious and say that boards are often far from unified. In fact, as you will know, boards are sometimes disunited and even downright quarrelsome. This, though, is of course not what is meant by the question.

The term 'unified board' means a board where all the directors, both executive and non-executive, have the same legal rights and responsibilities. Each is responsible for the operations of the company and the actions of the board. The directors may choose to divide up their responsibilities, for example by setting up board committees, but it is not a legal requirement that they do so. When they do, the directors as a whole choose the committee members, and can change the committee members. They retain overall responsibility.

The concept of a unified board has been under pressure in recent years. In particular, corporate governance codes, including the Combined Code, specify special responsibilities for non-executive directors. Nevertheless, the principle of a unified board is long established in Britain and it is intended that it continue. This was the position of the Company Law Review Steering Group and it will almost certainly be reflected in the next Companies Act. It must be a matter of opinion but many people consider that a unified board is a source of strength. Some people, perhaps the same ones, regret the trend towards non-executive directors policing the executive directors.

96   How are the chairman and managing director chosen and does a company have to have them?

It is sometimes thought that the members choose the managing director and chairman. This is not the case, though it does sometimes happen in practice. In theory at least the members choose the directors, then the directors themselves choose the managing director and chairman.

A company can only have a managing director if the articles permit it. They usually do and Reg. 84 of Table A specifically provides for it. The precise role and powers of the managing director are a matter for the board as a whole. Occasionally a board will decide to have two or more joint managing directors. Similarly, the appointment of chairman depends on the articles. Reg. 91 of Table A states *'The directors may appoint one of their number to be chairman of the board of directors and may at any time remove him from that office.'*

It is not compulsory for a company to have a managing director or chairman, though most do. Sometimes the roles are combined, though this is frowned upon by the Combined Code which is for the guidance of listed companies. Some directors operate with equal powers, generally in small companies where all the directors know each other well (and are perhaps related) and trust each other fully. Some directors prefer to operate without a chairman (and therefore without a casting vote), instead operating on a consensual basis. Some boards operate by rotating the chairman for each meeting or by each director holding the position for one month in turn, or some such arrangement.

97 Does a managing director have any extra powers recognised by law?

In general the managing director's powers are those given to him by the board. The precise arrangements may vary from company to company and case to case. There is just one power recognised by law. A managing director has implied authority to bind the company in all contracts made in the ordinary course of business.

98 The number of directors has dropped below the number needed for a quorum. What can be done?

Reg. 90 of Table A says that the remaining directors or director may only act for the purpose of filling the vacancies or of calling a general meeting. The general meeting can of course be used for the purpose of the members appointing additional directors. These powers may not be used if there have never been sufficient directors to form a quorum. If there are insufficient directors in the United Kingdom to form a quorum, any member can convene an extraordinary general meeting. This can be used to appoint new directors and it is a step that can be taken if there are no directors at all. Finally, it should be noted that the court has the power to direct that an extraordinary general meeting be held.

99 How can I find out if a particular person is banned from being a company director?

A register of disqualification orders is maintained by the DTI. It can be viewed at Companies House and can be accessed on-line.

100 In practice how does a company operate as a director of another company?

Its directors exercise the powers. They come to collective decisions about what the company will do, or they make a collective decision that one of their number will act for them. One director represents the company at board meetings and votes. Any formal signatures (such as attesting the use of the company seal) are made by a director and stated to be made on behalf of the company.

101 Is there a prescribed minimum number of directors and is a sole director permitted?

It is a legal requirement that a public company registered on or after 1st November 1929 has at least two directors and this cannot be overruled by the articles.

A private company can have a sole director if it is permitted by its articles. Table A does not permit it. A sole director cannot hold the position of company secretary. Articles may of course fix any number as the minimum in a public or private company.

102 Is there a maximum number of directors permitted?

There is no maximum number unless one is imposed by the articles. No maximum number is imposed by Table A.

Restrictions on who can be a Director

103 What groups of people are prevented by law from being a director?

A person belonging to one of the following groups cannot be a director:

a) *A person disqualified under the Company Directors Disqualification Act 1986*

   This is available to the court on conviction for certain offences and is available in addition to any other punishment. It is only for certain offences and not for general crime. The maximum possible period of disqualification is 15 years. Disqualification is also available to the court as a consequence of certain behaviour involved in insolvency and on application by the DTI after an investigation.

b) *An undischarged bankrupt*

   The court may make an exception but this is rare.

c) *The company secretary if he is the sole director*

   There is no problem if there are two or more directors.

d) *The auditor of the company or any group company*

104 What groups of people may be prevented by the articles from being a director?

The key phrase is 'may be prevented' and there are numerous possibilities. Table A makes no restrictions. The following three examples are among those sometimes encountered:

- *A share qualification*

   This means that a director must own or acquire a specified number of shares in the company.

- *A nationality qualification*

   This means that only a British citizen (or citizen of another specified country) can be a director.

- *A residence qualification*

    This means that a director must reside in a specified area.

All sorts of requirements are possible and may occasionally be found.

105 Are there any age restrictions?

Company articles may provide minimum or maximum age limits but, unless they do, it is possible for a minor (a person aged under 18) to be appointed a director. Not many directors are minors and it is generally accepted to be a bad idea. This is because minors cannot be held legally liable for many of their actions and contracts.

Unless the articles provide differently there is no upper age limit for private companies that are not subsidiaries of public companies. There is an upper age limit of 70 for public companies and private subsidiaries of public companies, but company articles can overrule this. In any case, shareholders can appoint a person over the age of 70 provided that they have received special notice that includes the proposed director's age.

106 Can a bankrupt be a company director?

An undischarged bankrupt cannot be a director and cannot directly or indirectly take part in the management of a company. A director is auto-matically disqualified when a bankruptcy order is made. A court can make an exception for a specified company in exceptional cases.

De facto and shadow Directors

107 What is a de facto director?

All directors should be properly appointed in accordance with legal require-ments and the provisions of the company's articles. However, it is possible to be a director without having been properly appointed. Section 741 of the Act states *'"director" includes any person occupying the position of director, by whatever name called'.* The name given is immaterial. They may be known as governors or some other title, but if they do a director's job, they are directors.

Each case must be assessed on its individual facts but, for example, if a person attends board meetings and votes, he is almost certainly a director. If a person is widely accepted as a director by staff, customers and others, he probably is a director. Such persons will have taken on the obligations of directorship, even though they have not been properly appointed and not reported to Companies House. They may not know that they are directors and may not wish to be directors.

108 I use the word 'director' as a courtesy title. What are the possible consequences?

The use of the word 'director' as a courtesy title is quite common, usually with the permission of the 'real directors'. It may be done to please the person concerned and is often done to impress customers or other business contacts. It is a dangerous practice and the writer recommends that it not be done, but he has never succeeded in persuading anyone to stop doing it.

It is widely thought that *Sales Director* means a board member in the legal sense, but that *Director of Sales* means a senior sales executive who is not actually a director in the legal sense. However, this cannot necessarily be relied upon. Not everyone is aware of the convention, nor is there any reason why they should be. The use of the word 'director' implies that a person is a director. There must be a risk that a person using the courtesy title has taken on the responsibilities and that third parties can rely on his authority to commit the company.

109 What is a shadow director?

Section 741(2) of the Act states:

> *'In relation to a company, "shadow director" means a person in accordance with whose directions or instructions the directors of the company are accustomed to act.'*

This means a person who is not on the board but who tells the directors what to do and they do it. Such a person is not a shadow director if he tells the directors what to do and they do not do it.

110 Can you give me some examples of when a person is or is not, a shadow director?

It can be a very fine line. It perhaps most commonly happens to a person who is not on the board but is a major shareholder. If such a person gives instructions to the directors and they accept them, he will be a shadow director. Directors, of course, do not have to accept the instructions, though the shareholder may take steps to replace them. Perhaps the shareholder gives advice to the directors, and perhaps after exercising independent judgement the directors accept the advice. This would almost certainly not make the shareholder a shadow director.

There are other possibilities. To be rather flippant, a gangster running a protection racket and frightening the directors could be a shadow director. Professional advisers can be shadow directors, especially if the company faces financial difficulties, but it does not often happen. This is because they usually understand the risks and are careful to give advice rather than instructions.

111 What are the consequences of a company having a shadow director?

Having a shadow director is a bad idea. It is bad for the company, bad for the properly appointed directors and bad for the shadow director. Many of the provisions of the Act and of some other Acts apply equally to shadow directors as to other directors. The provisions of the Insolvency Act apply to shadow directors as to other directors and these can lead to a shadow director being personally liable for the consequences of wrongful trading. A person disqualified under the provisions of the Company Directors Disqualification Act 1986 commits an offence if he acts as a shadow director.

Alternate Directors

112 What is an alternate director and what are his powers and responsibilities?

An alternate director is only possible if it is permitted by the articles. This is covered in more detail in the answer to the next question as is the formalities of appointment. The precise powers of an alternate director may depend on the articles but Table A permits wide powers.

An alternate director does what the name suggests – he acts as an alternate to the director that appoints him. Regs. 67 and 69 of Table A specify:

> 'An alternate director shall be entitled to receive notice of all meetings of directors and of all meetings of committees of directors of which his appointer is a member, to attend and vote at any such meeting at which the director appointing him is not personally present, and generally to perform all the functions of his appointer as a director in his absence but shall not be entitled to receive any remuneration from the company for his services as an alternate director. But it shall not be necessary to give notice of such a meeting to an alternate director who is absent from the United Kingdom.'

> 'Save as otherwise provided in the articles, an alternate director shall be deemed for all purposes to be a director and shall alone be responsible for his own acts and defaults and he shall not be deemed to be the agent of the director appointing him.'

This means that an alternate director can do everything that his appointer can do and is personally responsible for his actions. Only one person can act at any one time and an alternate director ceases to act when his appointer assumes his responsibilities.

If the alternate director is also a full director of the company, he will have two votes at board meetings, his own and his vote as an alternate. They may be cast in different ways.

113 Who can be an alternate director and what are the formalities of appointment and removal?

An alternate director is only possible if it is permitted by the articles. It is permitted by Table A which provides that a director may appoint any other director as his alternate or any person willing to act who has been approved by a resolution of the directors. Special articles may provide that a director may appoint any person as his alternate and that the directors do not have the power to reject his choice. An alternate director is relieved of his position and powers when this fact is communicated to the directors by the appointing director.

An appointment is made by notification to the directors by the appointing director and, if it is required by the articles, a confirming resolution is passed by the directors. The appointment may be for a specified period or it may be an indefinite appointment. Details should be entered in the register of directors and secretary, and Companies House should be informed within 14 days on Form 288a. The register and form should specify the period of the appointment and the director for whom the appointee will act as an alternate.

Nominee Directors

114 What is a nominee director?

It depends what you mean by the term. Never forget the words of Humpty Dumpty in Alice Through the Looking Glass 'When I use a word, it means just what I choose it to mean – neither more nor less'.

Strictly speaking there is no such thing as a nominee director. The law does not recognise the concept of one person acting as a delegate director for another person. Nevertheless, it is a widely used term and you probably have a shrewd idea of what it is likely to mean in practice.

A nominee director may be on the board because of a contract or shareholders' agreement, or because of an informal arrangement that he will represent the interests of a particular person or group. He may represent a parent company, a major shareholder or member, the unions, a works council, one or more unpaid creditors or a local council, and there are many more possibilities. The formalities of appointment of a nominee director are the same as the formalities of appointment of any other director.

115 Are there any special dangers for nominee directors?

Yes, there are. All directors, including nominee directors, have duties to the company as a whole and to the members as a whole and, if the company has financial difficulties, to the creditors as a whole. There are other duties and in particular worker directors may take comfort from section 309 of the Act which states:

> 'The matters to which the directors of a company are to have regard in the performance of their functions include the interests of the company's employees in general, as well as the interests of its members.'

It should be noted that the reference is to the employees in general, not to just some sections of them. It should also be noted that the primary responsibility is to the members as a whole.

A nominee director must not put the interests of the person or group that he represents ahead of the interests of the members as a whole. It can be a fine line calling for individual interpretation. It is sometimes argued that serving the interests of a particular group is in the interests of the members as a whole. For example, a contented workforce and well-informed creditors may well be in the interests of the members, but reliance on this should not be taken past the point of what is reasonable.

116 Can you give a practical example of how a nominee director might get it wrong?

I will do better than that and give two practical examples.

Scenario 1 – Failing to stand up to the directors of a parent company

John is finance director of ABC Ltd, which is 90 per cent owned by XYZ Ltd. ABC Ltd is profitable and soundly financed. In fact it has a million pounds in the bank and an unused borrowing facility of two million pounds. XYZ

Ltd, on the other hand, is unprofitable and faces financial difficulties. John receives a telephone call from Jenny the finance director of XYZ Ltd instructing him to pay over all the money that he can lay his hands on. John immediately sends three million pounds to XYZ Ltd. Shortly afterwards XYZ Ltd goes into insolvent liquidation. The three million pound loan is valueless and as a result ABC Ltd also goes into insolvent liquidation.

John has wrongly put the interests of his company behind the interests of the company that he represented. The creditors of ABC Ltd will not get paid in full and the shareholders of ABC Ltd (including the 10 per cent who are outsiders) will lose money. The consequences for John could be very serious.

Scenario 2 – Putting the interests of one group of workers ahead of duty to the company

Susan is a director of ABC Ltd and represents the interests of the factory employees on the board. The directors reluctantly decide that redundancies in the factory are necessary. They agree that they will work out precise proposals and discuss them with the people involved in a months time, but that meanwhile confidentiality is very important. Susan immediately tells the factory workers who promptly commence a damaging strike. This is not in the interests of the members and it is not in the interests of the employees who are not employed in the factory. Susan has failed in her first duty to the company and its members as a whole.

Appointment

117 How are directors appointed?

As explained elsewhere, it is possible for a person to be a de facto director without having been properly appointed. Such a director is either a de facto director or a shadow director. This is most definitely not recommended. Directors should be properly appointed in accordance with the law and the articles, and this is what does happen in the great majority of cases.

118 How are the first directors appointed?

The first directors are chosen by the subscribers to the memorandum. Their names, disclosable personal details and consent signatures must be on form 10 which is submitted to the Registrar of Companies as part of the process of registering a company. These first directors automatically take office as soon as the company is registered by the Registrar.

119 What part does the law play in the appointment of directors?

The law plays very little part, leaving it to the provisions of the articles. However, it is significant in three areas:

1. It directs how the first directors are appointed.

2. It provides that in a public company two or more prospective directors cannot be proposed with a single resolution, unless this is unanimously agreed by the meeting. This enables the members to choose individually rather than be confronted with an all or none decision.

3. A director aged 70 or more cannot be appointed a director of a public company or a private subsidiary of a public company, unless the shareholders have received special notice that specified his age. Articles may remove this requirement.

Of course a person disqualified by law (such as a person disqualified under the Directors Disqualification Act 1986) cannot properly be made a director.

120 What part do the articles play in the appointment of directors?

Subject to the few legal restrictions, articles govern the appointment of directors. The provisions of Table A are very widely adopted but many variations are possible and sometimes encountered.

121 What does Table A say about how members appoint directors?

Regulation 78 of Table A states:

> 'Subject as aforesaid, the company may by ordinary resolution appoint a person who is willing to act to be a director either to fill a vacancy or as an additional director and may also determine the rotation in which any additional directors are to retire.'

An ordinary resolution is a simple majority of votes cast on the day and this is the method most commonly adopted. Appointment of directors by the members is usually done at an annual general meeting but it can be done at an extraordinary general meeting.

122 What else does Table A say about the appointment of directors by the members?

Table A takes steps to limit the scope of members to ambush directors at or shortly before a general meeting. Other than for a person proposed by the directors, notice of a proposed appointment must be given to the company, together with details of the proposed director and evidence of his willingness to be appointed. Regulation 76 of Table A states:

> 'No person other than a director retiring by rotation shall be appointed or reappointed a director at any general meeting unless:
>
> a)   he is recommended by the directors; or
>
> b)   not less than fourteen nor more than thirty-five clear days before the date appointed for the meeting, notice executed by a member qualified to vote at the meeting has been given to the company of the intention to propose that person for appointment or reappointment stating the particulars which would, if he were so appointed or reappointed, be required to be included in the company's register of directors together with notice executed by that person of his willingness to be appointed or reappointed.'

123 What does Table A say about notice to the members of a resolution to propose a director?

Notice of between seven and 28 clear days must be given to all who are entitled to receive notice of the meeting. This is necessary unless the proposed person is recommended by the directors or is retiring by rotation. The notice must include the particulars of the proposed director that must (if the appointment is made) be entered in the register of directors.

124 Can the directors appoint a director?

They can if Table A applies. Regulation 79 provides that the directors may appoint a director to fill a casual vacancy or as an additional director. They may do this up to any maximum number of directors fixed by the articles. Table A does not specify any maximum number of directors. Regulation 79 also provides that any director appointed by the directors may serve only until the next annual general meeting, at which he may offer himself to the members for election.

125 What steps should be taken on the appointment of a new director?

The register of directors and secretaries must be amended and Companies House must be informed within 14 days of the appointment. If the director (or his spouse or children aged under 18) has notifiable interests in shares or debentures, appropriate notification must be given by the director to the company. It may be necessary to notify the bank and the bank mandate may need to be amended. Other notifications should be considered.

126 We forgot to notify Companies House of my appointment as director. What should we do and am I a director?

The answer is the same as the answer to question 175 which relates to the failure to notify Companies House of the appointment of a company secretary.

Resignation, retirement and removal

127 What are the rules about a director's resignation?

A director may resign at any time, either with immediate effect or from a specified future date. Company articles may specify details of how the resignation must be made but, unless they do, communication to the company is all that is required. It is good practice for the resignation to be in writing but, unless the articles say differently, it is not a requirement and an oral resignation will be valid. Once given, resignation cannot be withdrawn without the consent of the company.

128 I have resigned as a director but the other directors refuse to accept my resignation and they have just included me as a director on the annual return. Am I a director?

Unless there is some unusual provision in the articles you are not a director. Unless you specified some other date, you ceased to be a director as soon as your resignation was communicated to the company. The directors should have ensured that Companies House was notified that you had ceased to be a director and they should have done so within 14 days. They should not have included you as a director on the annual return.

129 I have heard that a director must step down on reaching the age of 70. Is this correct?

In general no, though a retiring age of 70 (or any other age) may be stip-ulated by company articles. The Act provides that a director of a public company, or a private subsidiary of a public company, must retire at the AGM following his 70th birthday. He may offer himself for re-election on a resolution with special notice, and the members may re-elect him having been given notice of his date of birth. Company articles may override the requirement of a director to retire at the age of 70.

130 Today is 7th September. I resigned as a director on 30th June with effect from 31st December. What are my rights and responsibilities until 31st December?

You are a director until 31st December and you have full rights and responsibilities until that date. The other directors must recognise your position and must, for example, allow you to participate in board meetings.

131 What are the rules about retirement of directors by rotation?

The Act does not require retirement by rotation but Table A provides for it and it is very commonly a requirement of the articles. Regulations 73 to 75 of Table A provide as follows:

> 'At the first annual general meeting all the directors shall retire from office, and at every subsequent annual general meeting one-third of the directors who are subject to retirement by rotation or, if their number is not three or a multiple of three, the number nearest to one-third shall retire from office; but, if there is only one director who is subject to retirement by rotation, he shall retire.'

> 'Subject to the provisions of the Act, the directors to retire by rotation shall be those who have been longest in office since their last appointment or reappointment, but as between persons who became or were last reappointed directors on the same day those to retire shall (unless they otherwise agree among themselves) be determined by lot.'

> 'If the company, at the meeting at which a director retires by rotation, does not fill the vacancy the retiring director shall, if willing to act, be deemed to have been reappointed unless at the meeting it is resolved not to fill the vacancy or unless a resolution for the reappointment of the director is put to the meeting and lost.'

132 Is it possible for the articles to rule out retirement by rotation so that directors serve for life or until they resign, become disqualified or are removed?

Yes, it is and it is not uncommon. It is a solution to a problem posed when a private company adopts an elective resolution to not hold annual general meetings.

133 Does Table A specify events which lead to loss of office by a director?

Yes, it does. In addition to circumstances described in the answers to other questions, Table A deals with three circumstances:

a)   *The director makes any arrangement or composition with his creditors generally.* This is in addition to formal bankruptcy as prescribed by law.

b)   *Mental disorder.* This is obviously very sad and it is important that the precise wording be noted. Acting strangely is not by itself sufficient, which is just as well or a large number of directors might be relieved of their offices. The precise wording is:

'he is, or may be, suffering from mental disorder and either:

i)   *he is admitted to hospital in pursuance of an application for admission for treatment under the Mental Health Act 1983 or, in Scotland, an application for admission under the Mental Health (Scotland) Act 1960, or*

ii)   *an order is made by a court having jurisdiction (whether in the United Kingdom or elsewhere) in matters concerning mental disorder for his detention or for the appointment of a receiver, curator bonis or other person to exercise powers with respect to his property or affairs.'*

c)   *Absence without permission.* This applies if the director misses every board meeting for six months and does so without the permission of the directors. The directors may, but do not have to, resolve that he be removed from office. The way that this works can be rather uneven as between different companies because the number of board meetings held can vary enormously. Company A may hold weekly meetings and a director attending one out of 26 cannot be removed. Company B may hold just one meeting and a director that misses it without permission may be removed.

134 May company articles make other provisions for the removal of directors?

Yes, they may and a wide variety of provisions may be found, some of them rather curious. They stop people in breach of the requirements taking office or remove them from office if certain circumstances occur. There are far too many possibilities to mention but they include:

a) *Share requirement.* A director must hold or acquire a specified number of shares.

b) *Nationality requirement.* A director must be a British citizen or even a citizen of specified other countries.

c) *Residence requirement.* A director must reside in a specified area such as, for example, the counties of Norfolk, Suffolk, Cambridgeshire and Essex.

Some of the requirements may be very controversial, at least to people who do not agree with them. A director's sex may be a requirement and so may a requirement that he be teetotal.

Restrictions in the articles can only be changed by a 75 per cent majority so it does not follow that a simple majority of the members can override a requirement.

135 Can a director be removed from office by a vote of the directors?

This can only happen if it is permitted by the articles. It is not provided for by the Act and it is not provided for by Table A. However, such provision is invariably made in the articles of listed companies and quite often made in the articles of other companies. In the absence of provision in the articles a director can only be removed by a vote of the members at an AGM or at an extraordinary general meeting.

136 What are the powers of the courts to ban a person from being a director?

A disqualification order may ban a person from being a director, and from directly or indirectly being involved in the management of a company. A ban is at the discretion of the judge or magistrate and is in addition to any other punishment. A ban may be imposed as a consequence of any of the following:

a)   *Conviction for an indictable offence.* An order may be made against any person convicted of an indictable offence in connection with the promotion, formation, management or liquidation of a company, on its striking-off or on a receivership of its property. The maximum period of disqualification is five years in a magistrates' court and 15 years in any other court.

b)   *Persistent breaches of companies legislation.* This relates to Companies Act requirements concerning company returns, accounts, notices or other documents required to be filed with the Registrar. The breaches must be persistent. The maximum period of disqualification is five years.

c)   *Fraud in winding up.* The maximum period of disqualification is 15 years.

d)   *On summary conviction for a filing or notice default.* The maximum period of disqualification is five years.

e)   *Unfit director of insolvent companies.* The minimum period of disqualification is two years and the maximum is 15 years.

f)   *Disqualification after investigation.* This may follow a DTI application after an investigation. The maximum period of disqualification is 15 years.

g)   *Disqualification for fraudulent or wrongful trading.* The maximum period of disqualification is 15 years.

137 Does the answer to the last question mean that some people convicted of very serious crimes cannot be banned from being a director?

Yes, it does mean that.

138 What is the procedure for the removal of a director by the members at an extraordinary general meeting?

The steps are as follows:

1. Members holding at least 10 per cent of the paid up share capital (or having 10 per cent of the voting rights if there is no share capital) may requisition an extraordinary general meeting. They must specify the wording of resolutions to be considered at the meeting and these can include the removal of one or more directors.

2. The company must give a copy of the resolution to the director affected.

3. The directors must within 28 days of receipt of the requisition call a meeting giving at least 21 clear days notice. Table A provides that a meeting requisitioned by the members must be held within eight weeks of receipt of the requisition by the directors.

4. The director affected may write to the members stating his case. This must be circulated by the company at the company's expense.

5. The director affected may attend the meeting and speak on the resolution to remove him.

6. The matter is decided by a vote of the members on an ordinary resolution.

139 What is the procedure if the resolution to remove a director is to be considered at an AGM?

The procedure is similar to the one described in the answer to the previous question. However, the requisitionists specify that the resolution must be considered at the next AGM, whenever it is. This avoids the expense of an extraordinary general meeting. If, after receipt of the notice, the directors call an AGM for less than 28 days thereafter, the notice is still valid. If notice of the AGM has already been sent, the directors must advertise at least 21 days before the date of the meeting.

140 Is it always one share one vote on an ordinary resolution of the members to remove a director?

No, this is not always the case. It is one share one vote unless the articles stipulate otherwise. It is possible for articles to provide for some form of weighted voting, with some shares carrying more votes than others. An extreme example of this was upheld in *Bushell v Faith*. In this case articles gave a director's shares extra votes on a resolution to remove him as a director. There is nothing in statute or common law to prescribe equality. In a company limited by guarantee it is one member one vote and weighted voting is not possible.

141 Can a director be removed by means of a written resolution of the members?

No, he cannot. This would deprive him of his rights to make written representations to the members and to speak on the resolution at the meeting.

142 Can the members be prevented from removing a director?

No, they cannot. The Act provides that a director may be removed by an ordinary resolution of the members. This takes precedence over anything to the contrary in the articles or an agreement with the director. Such an agreement may provide for compensation for loss of office.

Strictly speaking an exception should be mentioned, though any director affected will be very elderly. The exception is a life director of a private company who held office on 18th July 1945.

143 I control 51 per cent of the votes at a general meeting of the company. I think that women who wear trousers should not be company directors and a woman director will not heed my request to stop wearing trousers. Can I requisition an extraordinary meeting and vote her off the board?

Yes, you can, though many people would think you unreasonable. It is just possible that the director concerned may have a remedy under section 459 of the Act which relates to unfair prejudice. This is only possible if she is a member of the company or a person to whom shares have been transferred or transmitted.

Payment, expenses and service contract

144 Must a director be paid?

There is no presumption in company law that a director will be paid. Some are and some are not. Remuneration, if any, is only paid as a consequence of an agreement between the director and the company.

An executive director is an employee and is therefore presumably entitled to the minimum wage, though this has not been properly tested. A non-executive director is not an employee and the minimum wage is therefore not applicable. An interesting but untested point is the position in a company with just one director who is an executive director, but who opts not to be paid. Perhaps he is a sole or major shareholder and takes his reward in the form of dividends. It is possible that an offence is committed if he is not paid the minimum wage.

145 Who determines the directors' fees (if any) and terms of their contracts (if any)?

It all depends on the articles. Regulation 82 of Table A states:

> 'The directors shall be entitled to such remuneration as the company may by ordinary resolution determine and, unless the resolution provides otherwise, the remuneration shall be deemed to accrue from day to day.'

This can be cumbersome (at least from the point of view of the directors) because the members must be asked every year, or at least whenever the basis of remuneration changes. For this reason different arrangements are often specified in articles. There are numerous variations but remuneration and the terms of directors' service contracts are often a matter for a decision of the directors as a whole.

146 Do the Inland Revenue and others treat the remuneration of executive directors and non-executive directors in the same way?

No, they do not. The writer is not qualified to speak for the Inland Revenue but it is fair to say that the remuneration of executive directors is classed as salary. This means that tax is deducted through the PAYE system. It also means that they are treated as employees for national insurance purposes and that their companies must pay employers' national insurance contributions. The fact that the remuneration of executive directors is treated as salary also has pension implications.

Non-executive directors receive fees rather than salaries. This means that they are classed as self-employed by the Inland Revenue and that tax is not deducted through the PAYE system. This also has national insurance and pension implications.

147 What part of a director's fee is payable to a director who resigns part-way through a year?

It depends on the articles. Regulation 82 of Table A provides that unless the members decide otherwise, remuneration shall be deemed to accrue from day to day. This principle is incorporated into the articles of many companies, but of course not all companies.

If the principle does apply, if a director is to receive £10,000 for each calendar year and if he resigns on 30th June, he is entitled to £5,000.

148 I am a director and the sole shareholder. Can I take as much money out of the company as I like?

The answer is yes, but subject to some important restraints and warnings:

1. You must not take so much money that the interests of creditors are threatened. In particular, you must pay dividends out of net distributable reserves and not out of capital.

2. It would be wise to carefully consider investment plans and the company's future requirements for cash.

3. Any other directors have the right, and indeed the duty, to participate in making the decisions and to act in the interests of the company.

149 As well as being a director I own all the shares. I want to pay out all the profits to myself as a salary or bonus. Will there be any problems if I do this rather than pay a dividend?

You can in principle pay yourself a very large salary or bonus, or you can take the money in the form of a dividend. The decision can be based on what you want to do but tax treatment, which may vary from year to year, may well be a factor. Despite this general freedom to do as you wish, due regard must be given to the following constraints:

- The correct formalities must be followed. Each director has an equal vote, even if you do own all the shares.

- Whatever you do the correct declaration to the Inland Revenue must be made and the correct tax paid.

- You must not pay yourself so much that the solvency of the company and the interests of creditors are threatened.

- You must act in the interests of the company as a whole. If you own 100 per cent of the shares there is not a problem, but there is if there is a minority shareholder. A minority shareholder would get a pro rata share of a dividend but no part of your salary or bonus.

150 My company faces financial difficulties. How much should this be a factor in setting directors' pay?

This is a nasty dilemma but let me start by offering my sympathies. A labourer is worthy of his hire and a director is worthy of his salary or fees. It is fair and usually good business practice to pay fair and competitive salaries and fees to directors. On the other hand, directors owe a duty to their company and its members. It is not in the interests of members to pay salaries and fees that result in the insolvency of the company, even to good directors for good work. The answer therefore, is that it should be a factor but by no means the only one.

151 I am a director. What are my rights concerning the reimbursement of expenses that I have incurred?

In most cases the relevant articles will be consistent with Reg. 83 of Table A. This states:

> 'The directors may be paid all travelling, hotel, and other expenses properly incurred by them in connection with their attendance at meetings of directors or committees of directors or general meetings or separate meetings of the holders of any class of shares or of debentures of the company or otherwise in connection with the discharge of their duties.'

'May' means 'must' if properly incurred and claimed.

This is suitably comprehensive and it should mean that directors can be reimbursed for all reasonable expenses incurred in connection with their duties. However, it is worth pausing at the words *'properly incurred'*. A bus fare and a cheese sandwich is one thing, but a chartered helicopter and a six course gourmet luncheon is something else. Of course circumstances alter cases and even these apparently extravagant expenses may have been properly incurred. Perhaps the representative of the Saudi Arabian government was being taken to the ceremony where a multimillion pound contract was to be signed.

It is possible, but unlikely, that the relevant articles are constructed in a narrower way.

152 Must a director have a service contract?

No, there is no such requirement and numerous directors do not have service contracts. An executive director is an employee and is therefore entitled to the minimum statutory employment rights.

153 I am an executive director and I do not have a service contract. Should I have one?

In one sense you are mistaken in thinking that you do not have a service contract, though you might not have seen it and you might not be happy with its terms. As an executive director you are an employee and all employees have contracts which, in the absence of an agreement to the contrary, consist of minimum standards fixed by law. These cover such things as periods of notice, sickness and paid holidays. Other things may have been informally agreed and effectively become part of your unwritten contract.

You probably mean to say that you do not have a contract that makes provision over and above this. It is probably a good idea that you should have one, probably good for you and the company too. Nevertheless, do not forget that its provisions may be designed to suit both parties and not just you.

154 I am a non-executive director and I do not have a service contract. Should I have one?

You are not an employee so you do not automatically have minimum terms like an executive director. It is unlikely that you would have forgotten something as important as a service contract, so we will assume that you are correct. Yes, it probably is a good idea that you should have a service contract. It would be good for the company and good for you that the details be written down and kept in an easy-to-check document. It promotes certainty and avoids the possibility of arguments. The act of negotiating the contract compels both parties to consider important issues that may not have occurred to them, or that they may have avoided.

155 Are there any limits on the directors' powers to agree the terms of directors' service contracts?

Directors only have such powers if they are permitted by the articles, but it is almost always the case that they are so permitted. Unless the company is a wholly-owned subsidiary, directors cannot agree a contract that is capable of running for more than five years. If this is possible, it must be approved by a vote of the members at a general meeting.

156 What things should be covered by a director's service contract?

'Should' is rather a strong word but the following might well be considered:

a) *Remuneration* – This should be considered in its widest sense to include bonuses, incentives, share options, etc.

b) *Pension arrangements*

c) *Company car*

d) *Notice period* – This should cover notice by the director to the company and notice by the company to the director.

e) *Duties of the director*

f) *Holiday entitlement*

g) *The director's rights in the event of ill health*

i) *The company's rights in respect of misconduct or inadequate performance by the director*

j) *Confidentiality* – The obligation of the director to keep the company's affairs confidential, both during the course of the directorship and after its termination.

k) *Exclusive services* – Whether or not the director is allowed to take other directorships and employments, or to work on a self-employed basis.

l) *Non-competition* – It is often specified that a director cannot work for a competitor for a specified period after the termination of the directorship.

m) *Expenses* – The basis on which expenses will be reimbursed by the company.

n) *The company's rights to the exclusive benefit of the director's endeavours* – It is sometimes specified that the benefits of any inventions, development work, etc, made by the director in his own time, shall belong to the company.

157 I have heard that long periods of notice are frowned upon. Is this correct?

Yes it is, though perhaps it would be better to say that long periods of notice for directors of listed companies are frowned upon. Two year rolling contracts used to be quite common but they are now very much the exception. The Combined Code calls for maximum notice periods of not more than a year, but with an exception for directors recruited from outside so long as they reduce to one year or less after the initial period.

The Company Law Review proposed a maximum notice period of one year for all companies, but with a maximum of three years for a director recruited from outside so long as it reduced to one year after the initial period. As is the case now, a longer period could be sanctioned by a vote of the members. This proposal may well be incorporated into the next Companies Act.

158 Is there a maximum period for which a director's service contract can run?

Directors may, subject to any restrictions imposed by the articles, commit the company to a director's service contract, so long as no part of it is capable of running for more than five years. There is of course, no problem if any part of it is capable of running for more than five years at the option of the company rather than at the option of the director. If a contract is capable of running for more than five years as described above, it is invalid unless it has been approved by the members in a general meeting.

159 Who can inspect directors' service contracts?

Every member of the company is entitled to inspect directors' service contracts without charge. This applies to a contract with the company or a subsidiary company. If the contract is not in writing, members are entitled to inspect a memorandum of its terms. Members do not have the right to inspect a contract (or memorandum) that has less than 12 months to run, or which can be terminated without compensation by the company within the next 12 months.

The Act does not extend this privilege to non-members but the Listing Rules require that the service contracts of directors of listed companies be made available to non-members for inspection. Furthermore, the Listing Rules require that certain contracts be made available that do not fall within the definitions given in the Act.

160 Where must a director's service contract be kept and who can insist on seeing it?

A director's service contract must be kept at the registered office, at the place where the register of members is kept or at the company's principal place of business in the country of incorporation. The public is entitled to know where directors' service contracts are kept so, unless the place is the registered office, the location must be notified to the Registrar of Companies. All directors' service contracts must be kept at the same place.

Members of the company may inspect the directors' service contracts without charge. There are two exceptions to this rule:

a)   where a contract has less than a year to run or can be terminated by the company within a year without payment of compensation; and

b)   where the director works wholly or mainly abroad.

There is no obligation on the company to supply copies. The requirement is to make contracts available for inspection by members, not the public. However, the Listing Rules require listed companies to make them available to anyone and not just to members.

COMPANY SECRETARY

The position and the role

161 Is it compulsory for every company to have a company secretary and might the requirement soon change?

It is true that every company must have a company secretary. There are no exceptions, not even dormant companies.

The position may well change. The Company Law Review Steering Group recommended that the position be made voluntary in all private companies, though remaining compulsory in all public companies, and the proposal was endorsed by the Government in its white paper *Modernising Company Law*. The proposal may be implemented in the next Companies Act. It is a controversial idea and the proposal has attracted considerable opposition. There could be a compromise with the position made voluntary for private companies that are small companies for accounting purposes.

162 Who chooses the company secretary?

The first secretary is chosen by the subscribers to the memorandum and is named on form 10, which is submitted to the Registrar of Companies with the application to form the company. Form 10 contains the notifiable details of the secretary and must be signed by him to show that he has consented to act. The first secretary automatically assumes the office as soon as the company is incorporated. Subsequent appointments are made by the directors in accordance with the articles. Reg. 99 of Table A states:

> 'Subject to the provisions of the Act, the secretary shall be appointed by the directors for such term, at such remuneration and upon such conditions as they may think fit; and any secretary so appointed may be removed by them.'

163 Who can be the secretary of a public company?

The Act states that:

> 'It is the duty of the directors of a public company to take all reason-
> able steps to secure that the secretary (or each joint secretary) of the
> company is a person who appears to them to have the requisite knowl-
> edge and experience to discharge the functions of secretary of the
> company'.

This duty only relates to public companies and could lead to criticism of
directors if an unsuitable appointment is made. In addition, the secretary
must be:

a)   a barrister, advocate or solicitor called or admitted in any part
     of the United Kingdom or

b)   a member of one of the following bodies:

   i)   The Institute of Chartered Accountants in England and Wales.

   ii)   The Institute of Chartered Accountants of Scotland.

   iii) The Chartered Association of Certified Accountants.

   iv)   The Institute of Chartered Accountants in Ireland.

   v)   The Institute of Chartered Secretaries and Administrators.

   vi)   The Chartered Institute of Management Accountants.

   vii) The Chartered Institute of Public Finance and Accountancy.

There are exceptions to these requirements and these are explained in the
answer to the next question.

164 Are there any exceptions to the requirement for the secretary of a public company to be a member of one of the bodies specified in the answer to the last question?

The requirement to be a member of one of the specified bodies took effect
on 22nd December 1980 and company secretaries in position were allowed
to continue. A person may be the secretary of a public company if on 22nd
December 1980 he was the secretary, assistant secretary or deputy secretary of the company. A person may also hold the position if for at least 3

of the 5 years prior to the appointment he held the office of secretary of a public company.

In addition, the Act states that the directors may appoint:

> *'a person who by virtue of his holding or having held any other position or his being a member of any other body, appears to the directors to be capable of discharging those functions.'*

This last point might seem to suggest that in practice the directors can appoint almost anyone, but there is the overriding requirement to take reasonable steps spelled out in the answer to the last question. In practice the directors of public companies almost invariably do make suitable appointments.

165 Who can be the secretary of a private company?

The choice of company secretary is made by the directors. The articles may impose restrictions but otherwise they have a free choice. The following points are relevant:

- The company secretary may be a director. However, a sole director cannot also be company secretary.

- The company secretary may be an employee.

- The company secretary may be an outside professional, such as an accountant, solicitor or chartered secretary in practice.

- The company secretary can be another company. However, a sole director of the company cannot also be the sole director of the company that is the company secretary.

- The company secretary can be a partnership. In England and Wales this has the legal effect of making all the partners joint secretaries. In Scotland it does not have this effect and the partnership stands in its own right.

- There are no age restrictions.

166 How has the office of company secretary developed over the years?

In Victorian times a company secretary had little ability to act independently of the directors and the position conferred relatively low status. A number of cases confirmed this and on one occasion a judge made the unfortunate observation that the company secretary was a 'mere clerk'. It was generally the case that the company secretary could not bind the company except on the authority of the directors.

This unsatisfactory position (from the point of view of company secretaries) gradually changed, partly due to accepted practice and partly due to developing legal decisions. In particular, the 1971 case *Panorama Developments (Guildford) Ltd v Fidelis Furnishing Fabrics Ltd* established that the secretary is the chief administrative officer of the company. This means that in administrative matters he has ostensible authority to contract on behalf of the company.

The company secretary is an officer of the company.

167 What is the relationship between the company secretary and the directors?

This is a very difficult question to answer, though it is possible to say what the relationship should be and often is. The directors should respect the company secretary, both for his personal qualities and the job that he does. They probably want to leave a lot of routine administration, such as the statutory registers and the minutes in his capable hands, though they retain ultimate responsibility. They should want the company secretary to advise them on a range of matters and on occasion to offer constructive advice and initiatives, even when not asked. This happy state of affairs is to the benefit of all concerned and is quite often achieved.

On the other hand the company secretary may not always enjoy the complete confidence of the directors. If this is the case the remedy is in their own hands because they can replace him. Sometimes the directors want the company secretary to do very little and prefer to take care of the administrative duties themselves. A company secretary who does not have a good relationship with the directors is in an unenviable position.

The relationship between the directors and the company secretary is what the directors want it to be. The answer to the last question described the increasing status and authority of the company secretary. Nevertheless, it is still the case that the directors prescribe the extent of the secretary's role.

168 Are joint secretaries permitted?

Yes! Two or more joint secretaries are allowed. If joint secretaries are appointed they have equal rights and responsibilities and each must be registered at Companies House.

169 Can the directors appoint a deputy or assistant secretary?

Yes, they can. Section 283(3) of the Act states:

> 'Anything required or authorised to be done by or to the secretary may, if the office is vacant or there is for any other reason no secretary capable of acting, be done by or to any assistant or deputy secretary or, if there is no assistant or deputy secretary capable of acting, by or to any officer of the company authorised generally or specially in that behalf by the directors.'

This means a deputy or assistant properly appointed by the directors, not someone who just starts doing the job. It can be useful to cover illness, holidays, etc and company articles sometimes contain provisions governing the appointment of a deputy or assistant secretary.

170 Does a company secretary who is also a director have an enhanced role?

The answer is no. A director who is also the company secretary has no extra powers to the ones that he has as a director. In particular, he has no extra vote at a board meeting. Some documents may require the signature of two directors or a director and the company secretary. Signatures attesting the use of the company seal are an example. If this is the case, two different people must sign. A director/company secretary cannot sign twice.

171 May the company secretary vote at a board meeting?

The answer is no. If he is also a director, he has his director's vote but not an extra one.

172 Can the company secretary insist on attending a board meeting?

Perhaps surprisingly the answer is no. It usually goes without saying that the company secretary attends board meetings, or at least has the opportunity to do so. Nevertheless, the directors can decide otherwise, though they would probably be unwise to do so as they would be cutting off what should be a source of responsible and valuable advice. In fact they could face criticism or worse if things went wrong. If the company secretary is excluded, the directors are required by law to arrange for minutes to be taken. There may occasionally be a good reason. Just possibly the directors want to decide the exact size of the secretary's annual bonus, but it is probably a very bad sign. Perhaps the company secretary should plan to spend more time with his family.

173 What should the company secretary be paid?

This is impossible to answer, though as the writer is a company secretary he is tempted to say a great deal.

There is no presumption in law that the company secretary is paid. Remuneration or fees, if any, are a matter for negotiation between the company secretary and the directors. If the company secretary is an employee, he is entitled to the statutory minimum wage, though most company secretaries would receive considerably more. Regulation 99 of Table A was quoted in the answer to question 162 but it is worth repeating here:

> *'Subject to the provisions of the Act, the secretary shall be appointed by the directors for such term, at such remuneration and upon such conditions as they may think fit; and any secretary so appointed may be removed by them.'*

174 What steps should be taken on the appointment of a new company secretary?

The register of directors and secretaries must be amended and Companies House must be informed on form 288a within 14 days of the appointment.

Consideration should be given to various notifications. Perhaps the bank should be informed and the bank mandate amended. Perhaps the pension fund trustees should be informed. Perhaps the appointment is so momentous that a press release should be issued.

It is a good idea for the new company secretary to take possession of the statutory registers, the minute books, the company seal (if there is one), the memorandum and articles and any other relevant documents. He should check that everything is in order and make appropriate enquiries if this is not the case. There are two very good reasons for doing this quickly:

- The outgoing company secretary may still be available and it is best to solve any problems at once.

- Any problems will clearly be the fault of the previous regime. After a time they will be seen as the fault of the present incumbent.

175 We forgot to notify Companies House of my appointment as company secretary. What should we do and am I the company secretary?

Yes, you are the company secretary, so long as you were properly appointed and accepted the position. You became company secretary as soon as this happened and you took on all the rights and all the responsibilities. An offence has been committed from day 15 onwards by the company's officers and that includes you. Fortunately prosecutions are rare so long as there are no aggravating factors, such as a fraud or the same person being at fault many times.

What you must do is send form 288a to Companies House now. It would be polite (but not essential) to accompany it with a short letter of apology. Do not lie about the date of the appointment. Although the chances of the lie being discovered might be small, it would be the wrong thing to do and could have unfortunate consequences.

176 I have just taken over as company secretary and things were not in good order. What can I do to put things right?

If your predecessor is still available, it seems reasonable to ask him to put things right. For various reasons this might not be practical or, of course, he might not still be available. Regardless of this, there seems no reason why you should take the blame. Perhaps your predecessor can find missing documents or supply missing information. If not, you must tackle the problems one by one. Perhaps the directors can help. Perhaps the auditors can help. If the minutes are not up to date, you should ask the directors for their recollections and produce them now.

It may be necessary to get copies of documents from Companies House, perhaps including copies of past annual returns. Certified copies of certain resolutions should be delivered to Companies House and these include any resolutions altering the articles.

four

Rights and duties of Directors 177-212

four

Rights and duties of Directors

Rights

177 Can directors delegate some or all of their duties?

Directors can delegate many of their duties but not all of them. This is just as well otherwise directors of large companies would get home very late at night, though of course some would say that this is what they do anyway. Subject to the articles, which are very unlikely to provide differently, the directors as a whole can delegate some matters to a committee of directors and the committee can consist of just one director. This of course is a managing director. Directors can also delegate to employees who are not directors. Directors should take care when they delegate as they retain overall responsibility. They should take reasonable steps to see that the employees (and indeed directors) to whom they delegate have the necessary abilities and integrity.

178 Are there any limits to the number of directorships that I can hold?

There are no limits imposed by statute. There may be a restriction, or indeed a ban, imposed by a service contract but, unless this is the case, you are free to go ahead. Two possible limiting factors should be kept in mind:

1.   You must disclose any possible conflict of interest to the boards of both companies.

2.   You owe a duty of care to all the companies of which you are a director. It may be a breach of this duty if you take on too many directorships. You should not take on more duties than you can reasonably expect to fulfil in a satisfactory way.

Some people do take on a lot of directorships and some are criticised for it. You may have noticed press comment relating to some high-profile directors. The late Mr Robert Maxwell was a director of more than 200 companies at the time of his sad accident.

179 As a director am I entitled to access to all the company's statutory records, minute books and accounting records?

Yes.

180 What right does a director have to call a meeting of the members?

The directors may at any time convene an extraordinary general meeting of the members and submit resolutions to it for consideration. They must of course give the required periods of notice of the meeting and the resolutions. This power vests in the directors as a whole, not just one or more directors acting independently. The directors must, unless an appropriate elective resolution is in force, convene annual general meetings within the permitted dates.

181 As a director I want to take independent advice on my responsibilities. Can I insist that it be paid for by the company?

I can understand that there may be times when you feel the need for this. It could be legal advice, tax advice, or advice about a possible insolvency and there are other possibilities. Advice is normally taken by the directors as a whole, but directors can be liable individually and may want advice on their individual responsibilities. It is not unknown for a director to worry that the board is about to disregard his views and do something unwise or improper.

There is not a general right for a director to take independent advice at the company's expense but you could ask your fellow directors. They might agree and in some circumstances they might be grateful later. On the other hand, the board may have some suitable procedure already in place. This is recommended by the Combined Code in the following terms:

> 'The board should ensure that directors, especially non-executive directors, have access to independent professional advice at the company's expense where they judge it necessary to discharge their responsibilities as directors.'

Duty of care

182 I hear quite a bit about the directors' duty of care. What does it mean?

A director must use reasonable care and diligence in the exercise of his duties. If he fails to do so, he may be liable to the company for his failure and have to pay damages. It is rather difficult to pin down exactly what is required because the circumstances vary so greatly. It is necessary to look at case law to build an adequate understanding of what is required.

183 Can you supply a sentence that best sums up a director's duty of care?

This is quite a challenge because there are so many aspects but: *A director must show the level of care that an ordinary person would take when dealing with his own affairs.* I would like to say that I thought of it but it is a variation on something that appears in many textbooks.

184 Would it be right to assume that the standards needed to fulfil the duty of care are the same for all directors in all companies?

No, that would not be a correct assumption. The concept of the duty of care is the same but circumstances alter cases and, to coin a phrase, size matters. A director of a large listed company may well be expected to achieve a higher standard than a director of a small private company. Of course there are certain minimum standards below which no director should fall.

185 Can the courts, when considering an alleged failure of the duty of care by a director, use hindsight and second-guess the actions of the directors?

They can but they are extremely reluctant to do so. So long as the director has acted in good faith, the courts are generally unwilling to use hindsight and say that it was a bad decision if things do not work out as planned. They will usually only do so if the judgement of the director was really perverse.

186 Is it necessary that, in order to fulfil the duty of care, a director should possess or acquire special knowledge?

No, it is not necessary. This is just as well because there are nearly two million companies and it is impossible for all directors to have special knowledge. Even if a director is an expert, he cannot be an expert in everything. A director need not show more skill than it would be reasonable to expect from a person of his knowledge and experience. Once again, circumstances alter cases. An accountant, for example, would be expected to show more skill than an engineer when it comes to matters of accounts, tax, finance and associated matters. An engineer, on the other hand, would be expected to show more knowledge and skill than an accountant in dealing with engineering problems.

Directors may place quite a bit of trust in the special knowledge and skill of their colleagues on the board, unless of course they have reason to doubt their competence. Directors should know their own limitations, whatever they are, and to know when to seek expert advice and pay for it if necessary. They should not take on too much and above all, they should possess and use common sense.

Tolerance and even encouragement of generalists may seem odd, but there is quite a bit to commend it. After all, it was specialists that designed the Titanic and specialists that steered it into an iceberg. Noah, on the other hand, was an amateur.

187 I have heard that the courts are requiring a higher standard of care than was formerly the case. Is this correct?

Yes, there is this trend though most people think that the standards required are not unreasonable. Indeed, some people think that more should be required. For many years the standards required did seem very undemanding, at least when viewed through modern eyes. Of course it might not have seemed that way at the time. In the words of the opening sentence of *The Go Between* by L. P. Hartley 'the past is a foreign country: they do things differently there'. A study of past cases will reveal decisions that might not be reached today given similar circumstances. This though does not always stop them being quoted as precedents by directors accused of a breach of the duty of care.

188 One of our directors has behaved badly and is clearly in breach of his duty of care. Does this mean that all the directors are liable?

Not necessarily so. It all depends on the circumstances. They probably are all liable if they acted collectively in doing whatever it was that went wrong. They may all be liable if they neglected their duties and let him do things without taking a reasonable interest. On the other hand, it does not automatically follow and it is perhaps true to say that it does not usually follow.

189 Should my company take out directors' and officers' liability insurance?

It is certainly something that should be considered. The practice of suing companies and their officers (especially directors) is on the increase, and in America it threatens to supplant baseball as the national sport. At the same time the extent of directors' duties has been widening and they may be liable to the public, creditors, employees and others.

Directors and other officers may be indemnified out of company assets (for both legal costs and settlement costs) in respect of an action brought by a third party, and for defence costs in an action bought by the company itself. There are certain exceptions and it is 'may' not 'must'. This is if the articles permit. You might like to check the wording of Reg. 118 of Table A which is given in the answer to question 191. Nevertheless, insurance may have its attractions. The following are among the reasons:

1. It may be possible to ensure the company's liabilities as well as the officers' liabilities.

2. The costs of reimbursing officers may be painful (or even crippling to the company). It may make sense for the company.

3. Officers may find it difficult or painful to negotiate with their company over what are reasonable costs. They may want to spend more than the company thinks reasonable or be embarrassed to press for what they want. They may prefer the certainty of insurance and to negotiate at arms length with an insurance company.

4. Company articles may prohibit or limit indemnity out of company assets.

5. Reimbursement out of company assets is only of value if the company has assets. If the company is insolvent, the officers are deprived of this safety net.

An argument the other way is of course the cost. Insurance has to be paid for.

190 I was a director of a company that is now threatening to bring an action against me for negligence. Can they do that and what will happen if the case succeeds?

Yes, it can do it. An action may be brought by the directors, the liquidator or the administrator.

Section 310 of the Act provides that no article or contract with the director can exempt or indemnify any officer or auditor for liability in relation to the company for negligence, default, breach of duty or breach of trust. Any article or contract that purports to do so will be void. So if the case succeeds, you will be liable to the company. If it fails you may, if the articles permit and Table A does so permit, be reimbursed for your costs out of company assets.

191 An action is being brought against me for an alleged failure in the course of my duties as a director of a company. Will I be indemnified by the company?

You may be indemnified. Reg. 118 of Table A states:

'Subject to the provisions of the Act but without prejudice to any indemnity to which a director may otherwise be entitled, every director or other officer or auditor of the company shall be indemnified out of the assets of the company against any liability incurred by him in defending any proceedings, whether civil or criminal, in which judgement is given in his favour or in which he is acquitted or in connection with any application in which relief is granted to him by the court from liability for negligence, default, breach of duty or breach of trust in relation to the affairs of the company.'

This means that a director can be indemnified against the costs of defending himself in the courts so long as he wins. It also means that he can be indemnified if relief is granted by the courts. This is explained in the answer to the next question.

It is now possible (but not a requirement) that companies indemnify directors in respect of proceedings bought by third parties, covering both legal costs and the financial costs of any adverse judgment. This does not include the legal costs of unsuccessful defence of criminal proceedings fines imposed in criminal proceedings and penalties imposed by regulatory bodies such as the Financial Services Authority.

192 What is meant by relief granted by the courts?

A director may escape personal liability if relief by the courts is granted under section 727 of the Act. The application will succeed if the courts decide:

    a)   that the director has acted honestly;

    b)   that the director has acted reasonably; and

    c)   that the director ought fairly to be excused.

The third point is a subjective decision made by the courts and it should be noted that the director must succeed on all three points.

A director can never escape liability for negligence under Section 727. This is because, by definition, if he has been negligent, he has not acted reasonably.

193 The answers to the last two questions are quite worrying. Is there any evidence that people are refusing to be directors and is there any prospect of the law being changed?

There is no real evidence that people are refusing to serve as directors. After all a directorship usually confers money and status, which are two powerful reasons for accepting an offer. Nevertheless, fears have been expressed that it could begin to happen. A few high profile cases resulting in personal bankruptcy for misguided but honest directors could make a difference.

The law could be changed to allow more relief for directors. At the time of writing the Government is considering the position and various options are under review. It is probably fair to say that there is no consensus on what (if any) changes should be made.

194 Will you give an example of an old case concerning a director's duty of care?

I do not think that we can do better than *Cardiff Savings Bank, Re, The Marquis of Bute's Case (1892)*. It has some very interesting features, and one suspects that in today's climate the decision may well have gone the other way.

Losses occurred due to irregularities and an action was brought against the Marquis of Bute, one of the directors. One of the factors supporting the alleged failure in the duty of care was the fact that he had attended just one board meeting in his 38 years as a director. An extraordinary feature was that he had been made president of the bank when just six months old. In his defence, the Marquis said that he had had no reason to doubt the integrity and competence of the company secretary and that he had relied upon him. The action did not succeed. The judge said "Neglect or omission to attend meetings is not, in my opinion, the same thing as neglect or omission of a duty which ought to be performed at those meetings".

The Marquis of course came from a distinguished family that provided an eighteenth century prime minister. His reputation seems to have survived the case because his statue occupies a prominent position outside Cardiff railway station.

195 The Dorchester Finance Case is often quoted in connection with the duty of care. What happened?

This is *Dorchester Finance Co Ltd and another v Stebbing and others 1989*. Unlike the Marquis of Bute's Case it is recent and the claim succeeded.

The facts were that two non-executive directors rarely visited the company's office and no board meetings were held. They often signed blank cheques for a third director to sign later. The third director misapplied the company's assets. All three directors were held liable for damages. All three directors were accountants and two of them were chartered accountants, so they should have known better and probably did. The defence of the two non-executive directors included the contention that they relied on the fact that the audited accounts were not qualified. One is tempted to observe that had that particular defence succeeded almost any defence would have succeeded.

196 I am an unpaid non-executive director so presumably all this nonsense about the duty of care does not apply to me. I am right aren't I?

Either this question is asked tongue in cheek or you have not read the preceding answers. Yes, the duty of care does apply to you and the fact that you are not paid is irrelevant. Directors take on directorships for various reasons other than money, including prestige, friendship, a wish to serve the aims of the company and an attempt to enhance the value of their shares. Whatever the reason, they owe a duty of care to the company. The fact that you are a non-executive director also makes no difference.

Fiduciary duty

197 What is meant by the fiduciary duty of the directors?

Directors are trustees of the assets of the company and they must not misapply them. At one extreme that could involve theft of the assets, which would of course mean a criminal offence as well as a breach of a civil duty. It can also involve such things as borrowing assets without permission and not declaring a conflict of interest. Breach of fiduciary duty can take many forms, some of which are reviewed in other questions and answers.

Directors are in a position of trust and must act in what they consider to be the best interests of members. A court will normally accept a genuine attempt to do this by directors. It will not second-guess the directors and substitute its own judgment of the best interests of members. This is provided that the belief of the directors was genuine and that they acted in good faith. The court will only decide otherwise if the directors' behaviour was extraordinary and that no reasonable person could possibly have believed that it was in the interests of members.

Directors must not put their personal interests ahead of those of the company. They may only do this if they have disclosed the facts to the members and obtained their permission.

Duty to act within their powers

198 What are the possible consequences if directors act beyond the limit of their powers?

Directors must not do anything beyond the scope of the objects clause in the memorandum, and they must not do anything not permitted by the articles. If they do, the directors may be personally liable to the company for any losses caused. There is a further risk that the act may not bind the company and that the directors may be personally liable to third parties for losses incurred. It may be possible to have such acts ratified by the members if they are willing to do so, either before the event or retrospectively. However, some acts can never be ratified. They include:

- A fraud on the minority.

- A dishonest act.

- An act requiring a special procedure (such as court approval) where the act has taken place without the special procedure being followed.

Substantial property transactions

199 I have heard that the Act restricts substantial property transactions with directors. What does this mean?

You just might think that substantial property means a large building. If so, please remove this rather flippant thought from your mind. In this context it means anything other than money. The aim is to stop directors and connected persons profiting by buying or being given company assets, or selling assets to the company.

With certain exceptions directors (or connected persons) cannot buy or sell company assets unless:

- the members vote to give them permission; or
- the true value of the asset is less than £2,000; or
- the true value of the asset is less than the lower of £100,000 or 10 per cent of the company's net assets.

The figure for net assets is taken from the last set of accounts laid before the members. If no accounts have ever been laid the amount of the called-up share capital is substituted. The restrictions apply to shadow directors as well as other directors, and they also apply to transactions with companies that are subsidiaries of the company of which the person is a director.

200 Who and what are 'connected persons' in connection with substantial property transactions?

The definitions in section 346 of the Act are rather wordy but they may be summarised as follows:

- The director's spouse, children and step-children aged up to 18.
- Companies in which the director owns 20 per cent of the equity by nominal value or 20 per cent of the voting rights.
- Trustees (when acting as such) for any of the above.
- Partners of the director, including partners in Scottish firms.

201 My company has breached the rules concerning substantial property transactions. What are the possible consequences and remedies?

There are no criminal sanctions for breach of the requirements though certain offences may have been committed incidental to the breach. The remedy is the power of the company to insist that the transaction be rescinded and the status quo restored. This is not an absolute right and the company may need to act quickly. The power to rescind will be forfeited if:

a)   restitution has become impossible;

b)   the transaction has been affirmed by a general meeting within a reasonable time;

c)   rescission would prejudice the rights of third parties who have acted in good faith and in ignorance of the breach;

d)   the company has been indemnified in full against any loss caused by the transaction.

202 Substantial property transactions sound rather complicated. Can you give some practical examples?

All the following assume (which is very likely) that the articles allow the directors to transact with an individual director and that the directors agree to the proposal:

1.   *The director wishes to purchase for £1,000 a company car with a book value of £3,000 but a real value of £1,000.*

     There is no restriction.

2.   *The director wishes to purchase a company car for £3,000 with a book value of £1,000 but a real value of £3,000.*

     It is only possible so long as the net assets of the company are at least £30,000, or if the members vote to give permission.

3.   *The director wishes to purchase for £90,000 a company asset that is worth £96,000.*

     It is only possible so long as the net assets of the company exceed £960,000, or if the members vote to give permission.

4.   *The director wishes to sell to the company for £1,100,000 a house that is worth £1,100,000.*

This can only be done if the members vote to give permission.

It should of course be remembered that there will be tax implications if a director buys or sells assets at other than the real value.

Conflict of interest

203 What must a director do when he faces a conflict of interest over a contract with the company?

Directors are required to declare to the board any interest that they have in a contract or transaction made by the company, or which is proposed by the company. The requirements are far-reaching and cover a direct or indirect interest. They also cover companies or persons connected to the director. This includes (but is not limited to) spouses, children under 18, business partners, and companies in which the director controls a minimum of (say) 5 per cent of the shares.

Of course very small contracts or transactions need not be disclosed. Materiality may be difficult to decide. A good rule of thumb for directors is 'if in doubt declare it'. It will not do any harm and may save a lot of trouble. The interest should be declared at or before the first board meeting at which the matter is considered. The Act provides that for certain types of interest a general notification to the company may be given. This advises of a director's interest and the notification will be valid for future transactions with the same person or body.

Apart from the civil liability, it is an offence for a director not to declare a material conflict of interest to the board.

204 What happens after a director has declared an interest?

This depends on the articles and as they may vary quite widely it is wise to check. The 1948 Table A prohibits a director from voting and his presence at the meeting does not count towards a quorum. Reg. 94 of the 1985 Table A is more permissive. It prohibits a director from voting but lists certain exemptions to this general rule.

205 I have just discovered that a director failed to disclose a material interest in a contract. What remedies does the company have and what might be the consequences for the director?

To take the last point first, the director could be fined. On indictment the potential fine is unlimited and on summary trial the maximum fine is £5,000. A court might decide that the director had breached his fiduciary duty and order an appropriate payment. The contract is voidable at the option of the company and the director must pay to the company any profit that he has made. However, what has happened may be ratified by an ordinary resolution of the members.

206 Will a disclosure to the board of a personal interest in a contract be kept confidential?

No, it will not. A director's material interest in a contract must be disclosed in the annual financial statements and it is for the directors to decide what is material.

Loans

207 Can a company lend money to a director?

This is prohibited except within certain limits and circumstances, and it can only be done if the memorandum and articles allow it, which they almost always do. The requirements are complicated but the following is a working guide:

- When not more than £5,000 is outstanding in respect of each director at any one time. Loans to a person connected to the director are included in establishing whether or not the aggregate exceeds £5,000.

- When the payment is a genuine and reasonable advance of expenses.

- Banking companies may make loans to directors and so may companies whose business includes lending money.

In practice the legal requirements are not always observed as scrupulously as should be the case.

208 To what extent can a company make loans to persons connected to a director, and who is a connected person?

First of all let us clear up the question of who (and what) is a connected person. The following covers the great majority of possibilities:

- The director's wife or husband.

- The director's children (legitimate and illegitimate) and step-children, until they reach the age of 18.

- A company with which the director is associated. This can generally be taken to mean a company in which the director and other people connected to him have a 20 per cent interest.

- Any person who is a trustee where the beneficiaries of the trust include the director or persons connected to the director, or where the trustees have a power under the trust to exercise it for the benefit of the director or connected persons.

- Any person who is the director's business partner or a partner of a connected person.

None of these are connected persons if they are also directors of the company.

A public company, or a private company that is part of a group that includes a public company, is not permitted to make a loan to a connected person. A private company may make a loan of any amount to a connected person, provided that the memorandum and articles permit it and provided that the director has declared an interest to the board.

209 Are there ways round the restrictions on a company making a loan to a director?

Not many and perhaps not any. In particular the following are not allowed:

- A subsidiary company may not make loans to the directors of its holding company unless the aggregate does not exceed £5,000.

- A company cannot guarantee a loan to a director made by a third party unless the aggregate commitments do not exceed £5,000.

210 What disclosure must a company make of loans to directors and connected persons?

The notes to the accounts must give full details of any loans to directors that were outstanding at any time during the year. The disclosed information must, where applicable, include:

- The fact that a loan was made or existed during the year.

- The name of the director or shadow director and, if applicable, the name of the connected person.

- The amount loaned.

- The amount outstanding at the beginning and end of the year.

- The highest amount owing during the year.

- Details of terms, any interest and any security.

Details must be given whether or not the loan or loans are in breach of the legal requirements.

211 Are there any restrictions on a director lending money to his company?

No.

212 Is it allowed for directors to borrow company assets?

Yes, it is allowed so long as the articles permit (as they almost certainly do) the directors as a whole to give permission. It should be remembered that the director will probably incur a tax liability, and that both the company and the director will probably have a duty to report the details to the Inland Revenue.

five

Statutory registers and Companies House 213-269

five

Statutory registers and Companies House

STATUTORY REGISTERS

General (including location and inspection)

213 How many statutory registers are there and what are they called?

Compulsory for all companies

- Register of members

- Register of directors and secretaries

- Register of directors' interests in shares and debentures

- Register of charges

Compulsory for all public companies (whether listed or unlisted)

- Register of interests in voting shares

Voluntary register

- Register of debenture holders

No company is required to keep a register of debenture holders, even if it has issued debentures. However, if it does so, there are legal requirements concerning content, inspection, etc. Companies may maintain other registers, either because it is a requirement of their articles or on a purely voluntary basis. A register of sealings is a commonly-encountered example. These are not statutory registers.

214 In what form may the statutory registers be kept and, in particular, may they be computerised?

The statutory registers are traditionally kept in paper form, either in bound volumes or in a loose-leaf system. Appropriate records may be obtained from a legal stationer. You could draw up your own but it would probably not be advisable. It is permitted for the registers to be kept in computerised or other non-legible form, so long as the system is capable of printing out written copies. If the company is large or there are many entries, this has obvious attractions. Company secretarial software is very good and may well be worth considering. The Act requires that, whatever system is used, adequate precautions be taken for guarding against falsification and facilitating the discovery of falsification. Common-sense precautions should be taken, perhaps including such things as keeping the registers in a locked filing cabinet.

215 Must the company be supplied with information for the registers or is there an obligation to seek it out?

Some of the information is inherently available. For example, the information for the register of members comes within this category. Some of the information is not inherently available and personal details of the directors and company secretary are examples. So too is the information for the register of directors' interests in shares and debentures. There is a legal obligation that all information that is not inherently available be supplied to the company, which of course does not mean that in practice it always happens.

The person responsible for keeping the registers, usually the company secretary, is not required to act as a detective in seeking out the information. Nevertheless in many companies the company secretary writes periodically to the directors (and perhaps to others) in order to remind them of their obligations. It is also good practice to ask the appropriate person if it is believed that a notifiable event may have occurred. Of course, in practice it is safe to make some changes without having received notification in the proper form. A director moving house may come into this category. The company secretary may well know and might even have attended the house warming party.

In some instances the register should definitely not be changed unless the company secretary has been informed by the right person in the right way, and he should not act on what he believes. An entry to the register of interests in voting shares comes into this category.

216 Are there any requirements concerning where the statutory registers must be kept?

Yes, there are – the first one being that all the statutory registers must always be kept in the country of incorporation. So, for example, the statutory books of a company registered in England and Wales must always be kept in England and Wales. It is not allowed to keep them in Scotland. The detailed rules are:

Register of members

The register must be kept at the registered office of the company, or at some other office, the place of which has been notified to the Registrar of Companies on the appropriate form.

Register of directors and secretaries

The register must be kept at the registered office.

Register of directors' interests in shares and debentures

The register must be kept at the registered office of the company, or at some other office, the place of which has been notified to the Registrar of Companies on the appropriate form.

Register of charges

The register must be kept at the registered office.

Register of interests in voting shares

The register must be kept at the place where the register of directors' interests in shares and debentures is kept.

Register of debenture holders

The register must be kept at the registered office of the company, or at some other office, the place of which has been notified to the Registrar of Companies on the appropriate form.

217 Do nearly all companies strictly follow the rules about the location of the statutory registers?

No, they do not, especially the rules that require certain registers to be kept at the registered office. Usually no-one knows and no-one cares, and the law in this matter is rarely enforced. Nevertheless, it is the law and the law should not be lightly disregarded.

If, as permitted, registers are not kept at the registered office, the necessary forms should be submitted to Companies House. If one or more of your registers are not kept at the proper place, you should be prepared to swiftly bring them to the proper place if required.

218 What are the rules about inspection of the registers?

Register of members

The register must be open for inspection for at least two hours during each business day. However, it may be closed for up to 30 days in each year so long as the intention to do so is advertised in a suitable newspaper.

Any member may inspect the register free of charge. Any non-member may inspect the register on payment of a fee of £2.50 per hour or part thereof.

Register of directors and secretaries

The register must be open for inspection for at least two hours during each business day.

Any member may inspect the register free of charge. Any non-member may inspect the register on payment of a fee of £2.50 per hour or part thereof.

Register of directors' interests in shares and debentures

The register must be open for inspection for at least two hours on each business day and must be available for inspection during the annual general meeting.

Any member may inspect the register free of charge. Any non-member may inspect the register on payment of a fee of £2.50 per hour or part thereof.

Register of charges

The register must be open for inspection during business hours, subject to reasonable restrictions imposed by the company in general meeting, so that not less than two hours per day be allowed for inspection.

Any member may inspect the register free of charge. Any non-member may inspect the register on payment of a fee not exceeding 5 pence.

Register of interests in voting shares

The register must be open for inspection for at least two hours during each business day.

Any member and any non-member may inspect the register free of charge.

Register of debenture holders

The register must be open for inspection for at least two hours during each business day. However, it may be closed for up to 30 days in each year so long as the intention to do so is advertised in a suitable newspaper.

Any registered holder of debentures or shares may inspect the register free of charge. Any other person may inspect the register on payment of a fee of £2.50 per hour or part thereof.

219 What are the rules about the requirement to provide copies of the registers?

Any person may take notes or write out copies during a personal inspection of the registers. There are certain requirements as follows for the company to provide copies or extracts.

Register of members

Any member or any non-member may requisition a copy or extract to be sent by the company within 10 days of receipt of the requisition. The company may charge £2.50 for the first 100 entries, or part thereof copied; £20 for the next 1,000 entries, or part thereof copied, and £15 for every subsequent 1,000 entries, or part thereof copied.

Register of directors and secretaries

There are no requirements for a company to provide copies or extracts.

Register of directors' interests in shares and debentures

Any member or any non-member may requisition a copy or extract to be sent by the company within 10 days of receipt of the requisition. The company may charge £2.50 for the first 100 entries, or part thereof copied; £20 for the next 1,000 entries, or part thereof copied, and £15 for every subsequent 1,000 entries, or part thereof copied.

Register of charges

There are no requirements for a company to provide copies or extracts.

Register of interests in voting shares

Any member or any non-member may requisition a copy or extract to be sent by the company within 10 days of receipt of the requisition. The company may charge £2.50 for the first 100 entries, or part thereof copied; £20 for the next 1,000 entries, or part thereof copied; and £15 for every subsequent 1,000 entries, or part thereof copied.

Register of debenture holders

Any registered holder of debentures or shares, or any other person may requisition a copy or abstract. The time in which it must be provided by the company is not specified. The company may charge £2.50 for the first 100 entries, or part thereof copied; £20 for the next 1,000 entries, or part thereof copied; and £15 for every subsequent 1,000 entries, or part thereof copied.

220 I think that the rules about access to the registers and provision of copies and extracts amount to a charter for nosey-parkers. Why can't people get the information from Companies House?

Having a company is a privilege, and having a limited liability company is a very big privilege. In return the law requires that each company makes certain information available to the public, at Companies House and by inspection of the registers. The short answer therefore, is that it is a legal requirement. In practice the burden is not usually onerous. Most companies have probably never received a request for inspection of the registers.

It is true that most of the information in the registers is available at Companies House and can be inspected and copied there. However, not all of it is. A further factor is that the registers may be more up to date than the information at Companies House. For example, details of shareholders are only supplied to Companies House annually with the annual return.

Register of members

221 What details must be kept in the register of members?

This is set out in section 352 of the Act. For all companies the register must show:

- The names and addresses of the members.

- The date on which each person was registered as a member.

- The date at which any person ceased to be a member.

In addition, the register must show the following for all companies having a share capital:

- The number of shares held by each member, distinguishing each share by its number (so long as the share has a number) and where the company has more than one class of issued shares, by its class.

- The amount paid or agreed to be considered as paid on the shares of each member.

If a company does not have a share capital but has more than one class of member, the class to which each member belongs must be shown.

222 Are there any other requirements concerning the content of the register of members?

The names may be kept in any order, but if they are not kept in alphabetical order and if there are more than 50 names, an alphabetical index must be kept.

No entry relating to a former member may be removed from the register until 20 years has elapsed from the date on which he ceased to be a member.

If the company has only one member, the fact that it is a sole-member company and the date that this occurred must be endorsed on the register. If the company ceases to have only one member, the fact that it is no longer a sole-member company and the date that this occurred must be endorsed on the register.

223 What should I know about joint names appearing in the register of members and what about nominee names?

The names must be entered in the register exactly as shown on the documentation submitted to the company. In particular, joint names must be entered in the order shown. This is important as the order of the names has certain consequences relating to dividends, voting, etc.

You may know or think you know the identity of the beneficial owner behind a nominee name supplied. This information must not be entered in the register.

Register of directors and secretaries

224 What information must be recorded in the register of directors and secretaries?

For both directors and secretaries

- Full surname and forenames

- Previous surnames and forenames

- Usual residential address

- Date of appointment

- Date of vacation of office

For directors only

- Nationality

- Business occupation

- Other directorships currently held or held within the previous 5 years

- Date of birth

Directorships in dormant companies, companies in the same group and companies incorporated outside Great Britain need not be disclosed.

225 I expect that I should know more about names and former names. Am I right?

Yes, you are right. First of all, married women need not disclose their maiden surnames or any previous married surnames. Also the former name of a peer (if different from his title) need not be shown. A previous name need not be disclosed if it has not been used for at least 20 years. Neither need a name be shown if it has not been used since the person concerned reached the age of 18.

226 I do not want to disclose my usual residential address. Must I do so?

Your reluctance is understandable as it can lead to junk mail and other unwanted consequences. Nevertheless, it is a legal requirement for directors and company secretaries. Furthermore, it should be your usual residential address and not an accommodation address. It must not be a company office unless you really live on company premises. The only exception is if you have been granted a confidentiality order. This is explained in the answer to the next question.

227 What is a confidentiality order and could I get one?

A confidentiality order may be available for directors, company secretaries and permanent representatives of oversea companies with a branch in the UK. Application must be made to the Secretary of State and be based on the contention that the applicant, or a person living at the same address, could be subject to violence or intimidation if the applicant's residential address is known. If a confidentiality order is granted, a service address (perhaps a solicitor's office) is supplied to the company for the register of directors and secretaries and also to Companies House. The real residential address must be supplied to the company and to Companies House but it is not placed on the public record.

You might get a confidentiality order if your circumstances warrant it and you have the sympathy of the writer if this is the case. Application must be made on form 723B. However, applications are rigorously examined and confidentiality orders are not given lightly. At the time of writing approximately 5,000 confidentiality orders are operational.

Register of directors' interests in shares and debentures

228 What is the purpose of the register of directors' interests in shares and debentures?

There is a requirement for all directors (including shadow directors) to give full details of shares and debentures that they hold in the company or in any other group company. Directors must also give full details of any options to acquire shares or debentures in the company or in any other group company. Furthermore, directors must give the same information concerning shares or debentures (or options to acquire shares or debentures) held by their wives, husbands, children or step-children under the age of 18 who are not directors of the company.

The purpose is to show the extent and detail of directors' (and their families') interests in the company and any other group companies.

229 Surely the register of directors' interests in shares and debentures is unnecessary. Why can't the information be obtained from the register of members?

In many cases all the information can be obtained from the register of members, but it is convenient to have it readily accessible in a separate register. However, it is not the case that all the information can necessarily be obtained from the register of members. The reasons include the following:

1. The register of members does not show options.

2. The register of members does not show debentures.

3. The register of members relates to just one company and not to any other group companies.

4. Information relating to family members (who may have different surnames) may not be readily identifiable.

5.   Directors, like anyone else, can use nominee names so that their beneficial ownership is not apparent. Their true beneficial ownership must be disclosed in the register of directors' interests in shares and debentures.

6.   Directors' stakes in an entity such as an investment club may not be apparent from the register of members.

230 I note that the obligations extend to shares and debentures (and options to acquire shares and debentures) held by spouses. What about partners?

There are no such obligations and it is interesting to note that the law was framed when the institution of marriage was in greater favour than is currently the case. A director may live with someone without benefit of clergy and not acquire an obligation to report his (or her) partner's affairs.

231 There must be some rules about writing up the register of directors' interests in shares and debentures. What are they?

A director is not required to notify the company of the grant by the company to the director of the right to subscribe for shares or debentures, and the exercise of that right by the director. The company is required, on its own initiative, to amend the register within three days of the event. A director is required to notify the company of any notifiable event within five days of the event or within five days of becoming aware of the event. The company is then required to amend the register within three days.

All the number of days referred to above exclude Saturdays, Sundays and bank holidays.

232 Is there anything else that I should know about the register of directors' interests in shares and debentures?

The register must be kept by all companies, not just public companies, and it must be kept even if it contains no entries. It can get very complicated and directors may innocently not comply with all their obligations.

For example, the 18th birthday of a director's child must be reported if the child owns shares or debentures in a group company.

Register of interests in voting shares

233 What should I know about the register of interests in voting shares?

This register is compulsory for public companies, whether listed or unlisted, and one must be kept even if it contains no entries. An entry in the register may only be made consequent to receipt of a notice and not made on the company's own information. Any person is required to notify the company when their interest in the 'relevant share capital' exceeds 3 per cent, and they are required to notify the company when their interest in the relevant share capital drops below 3 per cent. So, notification is at 3 per cent going up and 3 per cent going down. If two or more persons are acting together, it is colloquially known as a concert party. In this case the obligation to notify extends to each person involved.

There are a lot of detailed requirements but the above is a fair outline summary.

Register of charges

234 What should I know about the register of charges?

Every company must keep a register of charges, even if it contains no entries. In passing it is worth noting that the fact that it contains no entries may be very significant to a person checking the register. As well as the register, a company must keep copies of instruments creating or evidencing charges.

The register must contain details of all charges affecting the property of the company, and all floating charges on the property of the company. Detail in the register must include the amount of the charge which may be (and often is) 'all moneys owed to the chargee from time to time'. It must also identify the chargee and describe the property charged.

COMPANIES HOUSE

General

235 What is the purpose of Companies House?

Companies House is responsible for registering companies and maintaining the register. Having a company is a privilege and having a limited liability company is a considerable privilege. In return for these privileges, which include in many cases an absence of personal liability for company debts, it is deemed right that certain information be placed into the public domain. Companies House is the medium by which this is achieved. Companies are obliged by law to supply certain information to Companies House which places it on the public record. Anyone at all, for any reason at all, may inspect and copy the information. Companies House is also responsible for activities peripheral to this.

As is implied by its name, most of the information supplied to Companies House relates to companies, but other types of organisation must supply information too. A list of them is given in the answer to the next question.

236 What types of organisation must register information at Companies House?

The great majority of registered documents are lodged by companies incorporated in Great Britain under the Companies Acts, but these are not the only organisations required to file at Companies House. The others are:

- Oversea companies
- Limited partnerships
- Limited liability partnerships

- European Economic Interest Groupings

- Open Ended Investment Companies

- Newspapers that must be registered under the Newspaper Libel
  and Registration Act

An oversea company is a company registered in any place other than England, Wales or Scotland. Companies registered in Northern Ireland, Jersey, Guernsey and the Isle of Man are among those counted as oversea companies. If you use a spellchecker you will probably find that it forbids you to use the word 'oversea', but spellcheckers tend to have the grammatical attainment of an educationally challenged, American teenager. Parliamentary draughtsmen are for good reason rather pedantic and they hold that Norway, for example, is over one sea, not several seas.

237 What does Companies House say that it does?

The following is taken from a Companies House publication:

'Companies House is an executive agency of the Department of Trade and Industry, and has five main functions:

- the registration of new companies;

- the registration of documents required to be delivered under companies, insolvency and related legislation;

- the provision of company information to the public;

- dissolution and striking-off companies from the register;

- ensuring that companies comply with their obligations in connection with the above functions.'

238 What is the precise meaning of 'deliver to Companies House'?

The legal obligation of directors and others is to deliver documents to Companies House. Putting a document in a correctly stamped and addressed envelope and putting it into one of Her Majesty's post boxes is a very good start, but it is not quite the same thing. Post is at the risk of the sender and the obligation is to get it there. If timing is critical, it is the date of delivery that counts, not the date of posting. Electronic filing has the advantage of eliminating these possible difficulties.

239 Is Companies House efficient and does it give value for money?

The writer has filed documents and used its services for a long time, and he finds that it almost invariably gives a very good service. It is responsible for almost two million companies and it does everything with less than 1,200 staff. Yes, it does a good job and provides value for money.

240 I am a director who failed to file on time at Companies House. Will I be prosecuted?

The chances of you being prosecuted are very small indeed, but of course not nil. Companies House prefers to encourage compliance by means of education and persuasion and, apart from anything else, it does not have the resources to initiate a large numbers of prosecutions. Prosecution is more likely if there are aggravating circumstances such as the fact that there has been a fraud or an insolvent liquidation, or that you are a serial late-filer. In the year to 31st March 2004, 3,376 directors were prosecuted, though some of the prosecutions did not proceed when filing was brought up to date.

Prosecutions are a separate matter from the automatic civil penalties which will be levied if accounts are filed late. These are almost invariably levied and are levied on the company itself, not its officers.

241 I am not too worried about filing late at Companies House. Should I be?

Yes, you should. Although prosecutions are rare it is an offence and, furthermore, it is not responsible. Late filing can affect the reputations of the companies and people concerned. If you were a bank manager, would you be inclined to lend money to a company that did not fulfil its filing obligations?

242   What are the compliance rates for filing on time at Companies House?

In the year to 31st March 2004, 95.0 per cent of companies submitted annual returns on time, and 95.8 per cent of companies submitted annual accounts on time.

243   Our accountant looks after most things. Is it his responsibility to get everything necessary to Companies House?

No, it is not. The accountant is the hired help and the responsibility remains with the company's officers. In most cases the signature of a company officer is required, though an accountant can prepare documents for signature and send them to Companies House after they have been signed.

244   To what extent does Companies House verify information supplied to it?

Companies House does not verify the information supplied to it, a fact that sometimes causes surprise. It is the job of the Registrar to register information supplied, not to check it. A moments thought will show that checking anything other than a minute amount would be an impossible job. Companies House checks that all forms submitted to it contain an entry in all boxes that should have an entry, and it may spot that something is seriously incomplete. It may, for example, reject a set of accounts with a missing profit and loss account.

245   What is the relationship between the Registrar of Companies and Companies House?

The Act and certain other Acts require companies and their officers to deliver information to the Registrar. Companies House is not mentioned, but in practice the terms are virtually interchangeable. There is a Registrar of Companies for England and Wales (currently Claire Clancy) and a Registrar of Companies for Scotland (currently Jim Henderson) and the two Registrars have distinct legal responsibilities. The Registrar of Companies for England and Wales is Chief Executive of Companies House which operates in England and Wales and Scotland.

246 Which are the most commonly used forms?

Forms 288a, 288b and 288c relating to directors and secretary and then form 287 relating to a change in the registered office. Every company must submit an annual return every year.

247 What is the logic of the numbering system of Companies House forms?

Each form is numbered from the section of the Companies Act that governs the information filed. This can save a little time if you need to find something in the Act, which is a very long document.

248 How can I contact Companies House?

Companies House has three offices as follows:

Offices in England and Wales	Office in Scotland
Crown Way	37 Castle Terrace
Maindy	Edinburgh
Cardiff	EH1 2ED
CF14 3UZ	
Tel: 0870 333 3636	Tel: 0870 333 3636
21 Bloomsbury Street	
London	
WC1B 3XD	
Tel: 0870 333 3636	

Companies incorporated in England and Wales must file at Cardiff. Companies incorporated in Scotland must file at Edinburgh.

Companies House website is **www.companieshouse.gov.uk**

Filing

249 What are the different ways of filing at Companies House?

The methods are as follows:

By post

This is still the most common method of filing. Documents relating to companies incorporated in England and Wales should be posted to Cardiff and documents relating to companies incorporated in Scotland should be posted to Edinburgh.

Hays document exchange

This is a way of delivering paper documents to Companies House. It is a competitor to Royal Mail and only available to those registered to use it.

By personal delivery or courier

This can be to the Cardiff, London or Edinburgh offices.

Electronic filing

It will shortly be possible to file all documents electronically.

Online filing

By the end of 2005 electronic filing will be possible in over 90 per cent of cases.

250 Please give a summary of everything that a company must file at Companies House.

Information to be filed can be grouped as follows:

a)   *Accounts* – All limited companies are required to file accounts.

b)   *Annual return* – Every company must file an annual return every year.

c) *Details of directors and the company secretary* – This must be done on forms 288a, 288b and 288c.

d) *Other forms* – There are about 150 forms. The appropriate form must be filed if the applicable events occur. Most of the forms are never required by most companies.

e) *Resolutions* – There are eleven types of resolution that have to be reported to Companies House but most of them are unlikely to be encountered in practice. The three types most likely to be passed and reported are:

   • special resolutions

   • extraordinary resolutions

   • elective resolutions or resolutions that revoke elective resolutions

f) *Other information* – Other Acts require that in certain circumstances information must be filed. For example, the report of an administrative receiver must be filed. This is the responsibility of the administrative receiver, not of the directors or the company secretary.

251 What are the time limits for filing at Companies House?

Filing is a legal requirement, not a voluntary activity, and it follows that there must be a time limit for everything. The main time limits are:

   • *Accounts* – A public company must file within seven months of the accounting reference date. A private company must file within 10 months of the accounting reference date. Both private and public companies may claim a three month extension (using form 244) if there are exports or overseas interests, though this concession has been withdrawn for accounts periods commencing on or after 1st January 2005

   • *Annual return* – It must be filed within 28 days of the date to which it is made up.

   • *Details of directors and the company secretary (forms 288a, 288b and 288c)* – These must be filed within 14 days of the event.

- *Other forms* – Limits vary, but many must be filed within 14 days.

- *Notifiable resolutions* – 15 days.

252 Please give details of how electronic filing works.

In order to file electronically it is necessary to register for the purpose. All filing despatched by electronic means must be authenticated by (or on behalf of) the company concerned, and this is done by means of an authentication code. This is a six-digit code, which may be chosen by the company and notified to Companies House. When a document has been approved for registration the sender will be informed. If a document is rejected for registration, the sender will be given the reasons and a contact telephone number. Rejected documents should be checked and amended, then resubmitted. This may be done electronically or in paper form.

Electronic transmission may normally be done 24 hours a day, 365 days a year, though the service may occasionally be withdrawn for maintenance activities, etc. The date that a document is received by Companies House counts as its delivery date for legal reasons, possible prosecutions, etc, provided of course that the document is in a form suitable for acceptance and registration. However, documents not received between 7.30 am and 6.30 pm will not be processed until the next working day.

253 How is consent to act evidenced when a document is filed electronically?

Evidence of consent to act is required, for obvious reasons, when a person is appointed director or secretary, or as an authorised representative of an oversea company, and this is shown by means of a signature on the appropriate form. When the filing is done electronically it is necessary to give any three of nine pieces of personal information, and the fact that the person appointed has disclosed the information is taken as evidence that he has consented to act. The nine pieces of personal information are:

- Place of birth

- Date of birth

- Telephone number

- House/flat number or name

- National insurance number

- Passport number

- Mother's maiden name

- Eye colour

- Father's first name

254 The answer to the last question seems bizarre. Are you serious?

Yes, I am serious and yes, I agree that it is bizarre. Apart from anything else two of the nine pieces of information are actually given on form 288a, which notifies Companies House of the appointment of a new director. It is so silly that one is tempted to put 'bloodshot' as the colour of the eyes.

Now the case for the defence. Companies House does not know if a consent signature on a paper submission is genuine, so this is really no worse. Only a registered user can file electronically, so if a mistake or fraud is investigated Companies House knows who sent it. Companies House does not know who put a form in an envelope and posted it in, so perhaps there is greater protection. Nevertheless, it does seem extraordinary to repeat two details on the form and say that a new director's father's first name was Fred, and that proves that a person has consented to act.

255 What is the future of electronic filing?

Companies House has an e-commerce programme that by 2006 should allow all registerable information to be submitted electronically. This includes accounts, which present particular difficulties. It seems to be making a good job of it and one could only wish that certain other Government departments and agencies were as successful. Electronic filing started in a small way but take-up has increased and is increasing. It will in time become the norm and it is not beyond the bounds of possibility that in a few years time the option of paper filing will be withdrawn.

256   I hate filling in forms so I plan to send all notifications to Companies House by letter. Is this acceptable?

No, it is not acceptable. If a form exists for the purpose, it must be used. Anything else will be rejected.

257   Companies House forms include a box for contact details. Is it essential that this information be given?

No, it is not, though it helps Companies House and it is probably in your interests too. This is because it makes it easier for Companies House to get queries resolved. A possible negative factor is that the contact details are available to the public along with the information on the form. The contact details given need not relate to the person who signed the form. As a final and not too serious observation, it just may be a surprise to a few people but there is no law requiring a person or business to have a telephone.

258   How can I get hold of blank Companies House forms?

Companies House provides all forms free of charge, including free of postal charges. There are four methods of obtaining the forms:

By post

Forms can be ordered by telephoning 0870 333 3636, by fax or by letter to Cardiff or Edinburgh as appropriate.

Personal collection

Forms can be collected from any of the three Companies House offices.

Website

Forms may be downloaded from Companies House website: **www.companieshouse.gov.uk**

Company secretarial software

Forms may be obtained from approved company secretarial software.

259 Exactly how are resolutions registered at Companies House?

There is a form for a company changing its name but with this exception, which is in any case voluntary, forms for resolutions are not available and the resolutions must be filed on plain A4, white paper. Each resolution filed must be certified by a competent person and it is usual for this to be done by the chairman of the meeting that passed the resolution, but it can be done by a director or the company secretary. If the resolution alters the articles, Companies House must be given a certified, up-to-date, revised copy with the resolution. This may be in the form of a complete set of revised articles, but if the alteration is obvious and minor, an altered copy of the original articles may be sent. The alterations should be signed in the appropriate places.

260 How does the annual return shuttle system work?

In nearly all cases Companies House will send a shuttle annual return form to the registered office about two weeks before the anniversary of the made-up date of the last annual return. This is pre-printed with the relevant information currently on file at Companies House. The company may use this form as at the anniversary date or it may choose an earlier date. A shuttle form will be sent at any time on request.

The form should be carefully checked and if everything is complete and up-to-date, the form should be signed, dated and returned to Companies House with the filing fee. If the form is not complete and up to date, in most instances the form can be neatly altered. However, notification of a new director or company secretary must always be done on form 288a.

The use of the shuttle form is not compulsory and you may prefer to fill-in a blank form 363a. This will be necessary if you use company secretarial software.

261 What is the requirement to give details of members with the annual return?

Every company must deliver an annual return to Companies House every year. A company limited by guarantee need not supply details of its members with the annual return, but a company with a share capital must supply details of its shareholders. This must include the name and address of each shareholder, and the number and class of shares held by each. A full list must be supplied with every third annual return. For the intervening two annual returns a full list or full details of changes may be supplied.

262 What are the rules about the quality of documents to be registered at Companies House?

Companies House will reject a document if it cannot be successfully scanned, but it may well accept it if it can be scanned, despite a minor infringement of the technical requirements. Nevertheless, there must be rules and Companies House is permitted to reject a document if it does not conform to them. The main requirements may be summarised as follows:

- Documents must be on paper that is white or otherwise of a background density not greater than 0.3.

- Documents must be on paper with a matt finish.

- Each page must be on A4 paper.

- Each page must have a margin all around not less than 10mm wide. If the document is bound, the bound edge must have a margin of not less than 20mm.

- Letters must be clear, legible and of uniform density.

- Letters and numbers must not be less than 1.8mm high, with a line width of not less than 0.25mm.

- Letters and numbers must be black or otherwise, providing reflected line density of not less than 1.0.

- Documents must be on plain white paper between 80 gsm and 100 gsm.

Companies House requests that forms and documents be either typed or computer-generated, or be printed in black ink.

263 Must the existence of a shadow director be reported to Companies House?

Yes, it must be reported on form 288a. Of course in practice it almost never happens.

264 Are machine-generated or facsimile signatures on documents accepted by Companies House?

Yes, Companies House will assume that such 'signatures' have been placed on the documents with the consent and authority of the person concerned. An offence is committed if this is not the case.

265 How can I be certain that Companies House has received something that I have sent to it?

You can send a short letter and a stamped addressed envelope with the document. Companies House will stamp it and return it to you. The problem does not arise if documents are filed electronically.

Access to information

266 How can I use Companies House to obtain information?

Access to the information may be had in the following ways:

a)   *Personal visit* – this may be to Cardiff, London or Edinburgh. On-line access is available at all of the offices.

b)   *Post, telephone or fax* – Information may be ordered for despatch. In all cases the telephone number to ring is 0870 333 3636.

c)   *CD Rom* – This is published to show information correct as at the last day of each month. It contains all the freely available information for each registered company.

d)   *Website* – The Companies House website address is: **www.companieshouse.gov.uk**

e) *Monitor* – Documents may be ordered for delivery later when they have been filed.

f) *On-line access* – It is possible to have on-line access to the Companies House database. This method is favoured by large-scale users.

Charges are made for much of the information but they are reasonable charges. Certain information is free, though there is always a charge for paper copies.

267 What are the advantages of the monitor service?

Without monitor it may be necessary to check frequently to see if something has been filed, perhaps every day if it is important. Monitor allows you to specify the requirement just once and you know that it will be sent to you as soon as it is available. It may be particularly useful to a person who wishes to see accounts as soon as they have been filed.

268 Is on-line access expensive?

This service is called Companies House Direct and it is relatively expensive if you are an infrequent user. This is because there is a fixed monthly charge as well as a charge every time the service is used. However, the usage charge is less than would be paid if the information is obtained by other methods. This means that it is cheaper for frequent users and much cheaper for very frequent users.

269 I am interested in a company registered in the Channel Islands. Can I get a copy of its accounts from Companies House?

No. Inter-registry links exist with the registry in Northern Ireland, but not with the registries in Jersey, Guernsey and the Isle of Man.

six

Shares, debentures and
dividends 270-302

six

Shares, debentures and dividends

Shares

270 My company is limited by guarantee. Can I safely ignore the questions about share capital and dividends?

By definition share capital and dividends can only apply to companies that have shares. A few companies limited by guarantee have a share capital, but the great majority do not and it is now not possible to form a company limited by guarantee and having a share capital. So yes, you can probably ignore these questions. On the other hand perhaps your next job will be director of a FTSE100 company, and it might therefore be a good idea to have a look.

271 What is the significance of different classes of share?

Many directors and company secretaries will have played the game 'Monopoly' as children or perhaps as adults. They may, like the writer, have drawn the Community Chest card that states 'Receive dividend on seven per cent Preference Shares £25' and, also like the writer, first realised that not all types of share are the same.

If there is only one class of share, problems do not arise, but if there is more than one class of share, directors must pay close attention to the articles. Some types of share receive dividends of a fixed amount or fixed percentage, and some types of share rank before other types of share. There may be more than one type of preference share and they may not, or may, rank equally between themselves. The term 'preference share' implies that this type of share receives a dividend before any remaining profits are available to pay a dividend on ordinary shares. It is possible that a company may have several classes of share. Directors, advised by the company secretary if necessary, must pay close attention to the articles when paying dividends.

Preference shares may be cumulative or non-cumulative. If they are non-cumulative and if a dividend is missed due to a shortage of retained, distributable profits, then the dividend is permanently lost. But if the preference shares are cumulative, a missed dividend must be made up out of distributable profits made in the future. This obligation ranks before the payment of dividends on ordinary shares. Preference shares are deemed to be cumulative unless the articles make it clear that this is not the case. So the Monopoly player with the Community Chest card may get his £25, even if it cannot be paid at once.

272 How do preference shares differ from ordinary shares?

The title of a share can be misleading, though usually it is not. A share called a preference share may not have preferential rights at all, or it may have preferential rights in some respects but not in other respects. The source of the rights, privileges and obligations of a particular class of share may be derived from one of the following:

- The memorandum (though in practice this is rare).

- The articles (this is usual).

- The resolution of members that created the additional shares.

Preference shares almost certainly carry a preferential right to receive a dividend. For example, the holder of 100 7 per cent Preference Shares will receive a dividend of £7 per year. So long as the money is available the dividend must be paid, and it will rank ahead of any dividend payable on ordinary shares. Preference shares normally carry a preferential right to the return of capital in the event of the company being wound up, though this depends on the terms of issue. There may be more than one class of preference share, and the amount of dividend and the way that they rank between themselves will depend on the terms of issue. Preference shareholders normally do not have voting rights but, depending on the terms of issue, may acquire voting rights if a dividend is missed.

Ordinary shares do not receive fixed dividends at regular intervals. The amount of the dividends, if any, is decided from time to time. If the company does well, the holders of ordinary shares may receive large dividends and their shares may become more valuable. If the company does badly they may receive little or no dividends, and their shares may become less valuable. When the company is wound up, the ordinary shareholders get everything left after the payment of debts and the return of capital (of a fixed amount) to the holders of preference shares. The ordinary shareholders vote at general meetings, choose the directors and auditors, etc.

273 What is the difference between cumulative preference shares and non-cumulative preference shares?

The difference is what happens if the payment of a dividend is missed. If it is a non-cumulative preference share, the dividend is lost for ever and never paid. If it is a cumulative preference share, the dividend may be paid later, if and when the funds to do so are available. It depends on the terms of issue but the rights will probably be cumulative unless the contrary is stated.

274 What is meant by the term 'partly paid shares'?

Most shares are issued fully paid. This means that the successful applicants pay the full amount when the shares are issued. In the case of partly paid shares only part of the money is paid when the shares are issued. The remainder of the money is called up at a later date.

Sometimes calls are left to the discretion of the directors and may never be made, and sometimes instalments are at intervals specified in the terms of issue. Many of the so-called privatisation issues a few years ago were done in this way. British Telecom PLC was an example. A valid call must be paid even if the shares are worthless. In the event of financial difficulties the uncalled capital must be called up and used to pay the debts.

275 Can I buy shares using a nominee name?

Yes, you can and it is very common. There are many possible reasons for doing so. One may be a wish for secrecy or privacy. Another may be administrative convenience. It is extremely common, and perhaps even required, for shares held by stockbrokers, investment managers, etc. There has been some unease that requirements for beneficial owners to use nominees increases the isolation of shareholders from companies, and creates problems with such matters as voting and the flow of information.

English companies are not allowed to enter any notice of trust on to the register of members, even if they have been notified of the information. The position is different under Scottish law where such notice may be entered on the register if the articles permit. A company should deal exclusively with the body or person named in its register, even if the word 'nominee' appears in its name and even if the company knows or believes that it is acting in the capacity of a nominee.

276 What is meant by the term 'pre-emption rights'?

There is a general requirement under the Act that new shares to be issued for cash must be offered to existing shareholders in proportion to their existing holdings. Only shares not accepted by the existing shareholders may be allotted to non-shareholders. This is what is meant by pre-emption. The principle and details of this are covered by Sections 89 to 96 of the Act. Pre-emption rights apply to shares, securities that may be converted into shares and options to acquire shares. Pre-emption rights do **not** apply to:

- Subscribers' and bonus shares

- Shares allotted under an employees' share scheme

- Shares with limited rights as to dividends and capital participation

- Shares allotted, wholly or partially, for non-cash consideration.

The point of pre-emption rights is that they stop a shareholder's rights being watered down without his consent. For example, a person holding 26 per cent of the shares is able to block a special resolution. If enough new shares are issued and if the shareholder is not able to buy a pro-rata proportion, this right will be lost.

277 Are there some circumstances in which pre-emption rights do not apply?

There are the exceptions listed in the answer to the previous question and in addition, the memorandum or articles of a private company may over-ride statutory provisions concerning pre-emption rights. A private company's memorandum or articles may exclude pre-emption rights, or may stipulate that they operate in detail in a way different from the Act's requirements. In both public and private companies pre-emption rights may be modified or abolished if directors have been given a general autho-risation under Section 80 to allot shares. Such authorisation may have been given by the articles or by a special resolution of the members.

There are certain requirements of listed companies relating to pre-emption rights.

278 May shares be issued at a premium and may they be issued at a discount?

Subject to certain conditions shares may be issued at a premium, but they may not be issued at a discount. However, a company may pay a commission of up to 10 per cent in consideration for a person subscribing or procuring subscriptions for its shares.

279 What must happen in the event of a serious loss of capital by a public company?

There is a special requirement when the net assets of a public company fall to half or less of the company's called-up share capital. The directors must convene an extraordinary general meeting and they must do so within 28 days of any director becoming aware of the situation. The meeting must be called for a date not more than 56 days after a director became aware of the situation. The requirement only applies to public companies. There are no requirements concerning what, if anything, must be done at the meeting, and there are no requirements that directors make proposals to the meeting.

280 In what circumstances may shares be forfeited or surrendered?

Forfeiture of shares may be the ultimate sanction if a shareholder repeatedly fails to pay calls or instalments. It is only possible if it is permitted by the articles and the detailed provisions of the articles must be strictly followed. Table A does provide for the forfeiture of shares. Surrender occurs if a member voluntarily surrenders his shares and the directors accept the surrender. The directors can then deal with the shares as if they had been forfeited. Despite forfeiture the member (or former member) remains prima facie liable to pay sums outstanding on the shares at the time of forfeiture. There are special requirements concerning the forfeiture or surrender of shares in public companies.

281 Is interest payable if calls are paid late?

It is if the articles permit it. Table A does permit it.

282 Can stock be converted into shares?

The term stocks and shares is part of the English language but there are now virtually no practical advantages in having stock rather than shares. So long as the articles permit, stock can be converted into paid-up shares by means of an ordinary resolution.

283 Can a minor own shares in his own name?

Yes, but it is probably not a good idea. A minor may be a member of a company, but he may repudiate membership and the obligations of membership at any time before his eighteenth birthday or very soon afterwards. Such obligations may include the requirement to pay a call on his shares. If he has not repudiated membership by his eighteenth birthday or soon afterwards, he will assume the full obligations of his ownership. Although a minor may be a member of a company, there is no obligation on a company to accept a minor as a member. In practice most companies do not accept a minor as a member, although there are no problems with a nominee holding with a minor as the beneficial owner.

It sometimes happens that a minor becomes a member without the company being aware of the fact. In these circumstances the company may act if and when the true position becomes known, and it may do so at any time before the minor reaches his eighteenth birthday. The company may remove the minor's name from the register of members and restore the name of the person from whom he acquired the shares.

If the company registers a minor as a member whilst knowing that he is a minor, it cannot afterwards repudiate the decision. A minor who is properly registered as a member may exercise rights of membership, including receipt of dividends. Subject to any restrictions in the articles, a minor may vote at meetings. A company should not accept a transfer of shares purported to be made by a person known to be a minor.

Debentures

284 What is the essential difference between shares and debentures?

Shareholders own the company. The rights of different classes of share may vary, but shareholders have the possibility or probability of receiving dividends. When the company is wound up their capital, so long as the company is solvent, is returned to them.

Debenture holders do not own the company – they lend money to it and the debenture is a secured loan. The rights of debenture holders may vary, but they are rewarded by receiving interest rather than dividends. Interest must, so long as the money is available, be paid and it ranks ahead of the payment of dividends – even dividends on preference shares. Debenture interest is a charge against profit, whereas dividends are an appropriation of profit.

285 What charges must be registered?

Nearly all charges must be registered with the Registrar of Companies. Section 396 of the Act states that (in England and Wales) the following types of charge must be registered:

- A charge for the purpose of securing any issue of debentures.

- A charge on uncalled share capital of the company.

- A charge created or evidenced by an instrument which, if executed by an individual, would require registration as a bill of sale.

- A charge on land (wherever situated) or any interest in it, but not including a charge for any rent or other periodical sum issuing out of the land.

- A charge on book debts of the company.

- A floating charge on the company's undertaking or property.

- A charge on calls made but not paid.

- A charge on a ship or aircraft, or any share in a ship.

- A charge on goodwill (or on any intellectual property).

The list is slightly different for Scotland and may be found in section 410 of the Act.

Registration must usually be done by means of form 395, though in some circumstances form 397a or form 400 must be used. Registration must be within 21 days of the creation of the charge. Responsibility for registering the charge lies with the company that issued it. However, registration may be conducted by any party with an interest. In practice, it is nearly always done by the trustee or the debenture holder. This is because the consequences of not doing so may be awful for them.

286 What is the position if a charge is not registered?

If a charge is not properly registered, the trustee or debenture holder will retain rights against the company and the money becomes immediately repayable. However, the charge will not be valid against a liquidator or other creditors. There may also be the possibility of criminal charges. Proper registration with the Registrar of Companies constitutes notice to all the world and is why the appropriate records at Companies House are examined so assiduously in search of prior charges.

Dividends

287 Out of what funds may dividends be paid?

Dividends must not be paid out of capital. They may only be paid out of net distributable realised profits, either made in the current year or retained from previous years. It is an important distinction which directors must observe. Section 263 of the Act states:

> 'a company's profits available for distribution are its accumulated, realised profits, so far as not previously utilised by distribution or capitalisation, less its accumulated, realised losses, so far as not previously written off in a reduction or reorganisation of capital duly made.'

Precise interpretation of accumulated, realised profits can be very technical, but this is the legal requirement. Section 264 of the Act gives a further and slightly more restrictive requirement for public companies. Such companies may only pay a dividend provided that it does not result in their net assets being less than the aggregate of called-up share capital and undistributable reserves.

288 Do the same restrictions apply to the payment of interest on loan stock and debentures?

No, they do not. Payment of interest on loan stock and debentures is not restricted by the requirement to pay only out of retained, distributable profits. Such payments discharge debts of the company and are not a distribution of profits.

289 What is the procedure for declaring and paying an interim dividend?

This must be done according to the provisions of the articles. Reg. 103 of Table A permits one or more interim dividend to be declared and paid by the directors without reference to the members. All that is necessary is for the directors to make the decision, minute the decision and then arrange for payment to be made.

290 What is the procedure for declaring and paying a final dividend?

This must be done according to the provisions of the articles. Reg. 102 of Table A provides as follows:

> 'Subject to the provisions of the Act, the company may by ordinary resolution declare dividends in accordance with the respective rights of the members, but no dividend shall exceed the amount recommended by the directors.'

This means that a final dividend is recommended to a general meeting (usually the AGM) by the directors. The members can (and usually do) vote for the proposed dividend, or they can reject it and not pay a final dividend or amend the proposed payment in a downwards direction.

291 Please give me examples of resolutions for the declaration of an interim dividend and a final dividend.

Directors' resolution for the declaration of an interim dividend

> 'That an interim dividend for the year ended .... of .... p per share of the ordinary shares of £1 each of the company be paid on .... to shareholders registered at the close of business on ....'

Members' resolution for the declaration of a final dividend

> 'That a final dividend for the year ended .... of ....p per share (making with the interim dividend of ......p per share already paid, a total dividend for the year of .... p per share) on the ordinary shares of £1 each of the company being declared payable on .... to shareholders registered at the close of business on ....'

292 My company has passed an elective resolution not to hold annual general meetings. How can dividends be paid?

The simplest solution is for the directors to declare and pay interim dividends whenever it is wished that a dividend be paid. Subject to the money being available, this can be done at any time and more than once in a year. If this is done, no final dividends would ever be paid. Alternatively, extraordinary general meetings could be called for the purpose of declaring final dividends, though this somewhat negates the purpose of the elective resolution.

293 Shareholder A sold shares to Shareholder B at about the time that the dividend was declared. Which one gets the dividend?

In the case of a listed company it is decided according to the published rules. In the case of an unlisted company it all depends and it is one reason why it is important that the dividend resolutions be very carefully drafted. In an unlisted company the date for payment of the dividend is fixed at the time that the dividend is declared. Also fixed at the same time is the date at which names on the share register qualify to receive the dividend. This is obviously important as the sale of shares just before or just after the date may determine whether the buyer or the seller receives the dividend. In practice the parties in the purchase and sale of shares in a private company often fix the matter between themselves.

294 Is it necessary to pass a resolution to pay a dividend on preference shares?

No, it is not usually necessary. The payment of an ordinary dividend and the amount of the dividend is a matter of choice and a resolution is therefore necessary. Subject to the funds being available, the payment of a preference dividend according to the terms of the issue of the shares is a commitment of the company. The directors can just pay the dividends on the due dates.

295 What is a scrip dividend?

A scrip dividend is an issue of further shares rather than a cash distribution. Scrip dividends are sometimes attractive to companies because cash is retained in the company. Tax is payable on scrip dividends, but they are a cost-effective way of reinvesting dividends in the company. For this reason they are attractive to some shareholders.

A scrip dividend is a bonus issue of shares. The company must have sufficient authorised but unissued share capital, and such an issue must be permitted by the articles. Sanction by the members in a general meeting is normally required. Sometimes members are given the choice of taking a dividend in this way, rather than in cash. Furthermore, members may be permitted to give the company a standing instruction that all dividends will be taken in this way until the instruction is changed.

296 Is it compulsory to provide a tax voucher?

Yes, it is compulsory. It is a legal requirement that warrants issued in connection with the payment of a dividend must be accompanied by a document usually described as a tax voucher. Such a document must be sent to shareholders when the payments are made by means of bank transfers. A tax voucher must also be sent if the payment is of interest rather than of a dividend. It is now possible to send tax vouchers on an annual basis rather than accompanying each payment.

A tax voucher is a statement addressed to the shareholder (or stockholder) setting out the number of shares (or amount of stock) on which the payment is calculated. It must state the tax credit (if the payment is a dividend), or the tax deducted (if the payment is interest) and the net amount payable. In the case of interest payments, the gross amount payable is also shown and the tax voucher includes a certificate to the effect that the tax deducted will be accounted for to the Inland Revenue.

297 Is the issue of a duplicate tax voucher permitted?

Shareholders may, from time to time, lose tax vouchers and request dupli-
cates. A company may issue a duplicate so long as it is marked that it is
a duplicate voucher. No indemnity is necessary.

298 The shareholders want bigger dividends than the directors are willing to recommend. What happens?

Table A and almost all company articles prevent dividends being paid that
are greater than the directors are willing to recommend. There are very
good reasons for this. The directors know (or should know) the maximum
amounts that can legally be paid, they know what can prudently be paid
and they know their plans and the need for working capital. The shareholders can try to persuade the directors to pay bigger dividends, but if
they fail they should listen carefully to the directors' reasons for saying
no. They might be good reasons. However, the shareholders own the
company and they choose the directors. They have the ultimate power to
remove the directors and replace them with others who share their views,
or at least are willing to do as they are told.

299 Can a shareholder waive a dividend?

Yes, this is possible, though you might have difficulty in thinking of circumstances in which a shareholder might wish to do so. One example known
to the writer is a majority shareholder who is a director of the company.
He is very well rewarded by salary and bonuses and feels it right that only
the minority shareholders should benefit from dividends.

On no account should the shareholder just fail to bank his dividend, or
write to the company asking for it not to be paid. This would probably
result in him incurring a tax liability which would presumably be beyond
the limits of his selflessness. Instead he should complete a deed of waiver
and submit it to the company. Specimen wording of such a deed may be
found in a book such as 'Company Secretarial Practice' published by ICSA
Publishing Ltd, or perhaps professional advice should be obtained.

300 How should we respond to a request to issue a duplicate dividend warrant?

The advantages of paying a dividend by bank transfer include the fact that it is more likely to get into the recipient's bank account and that the company will quickly know if it does not. A dividend warrant sent by post may be lost, delivered to an out of date address or simply not be banked, especially if it is for a small amount. It is normal practice to indicate that warrants must be presented for payment within six months or returned to the company for verification. Some companies charge a small fee for this. There should be no problem in issuing a duplicate warrant at the request of a shareholder, though a check should first be made that the original has not been paid and a stop placed on the original. It is usual to first obtain an undertaking from the shareholder (if the amount is small) or an indemnity (if the amount is large).

301 A dividend warrant has not been presented for payment. What should we do?

It is tempting to do nothing but this is probably not a good idea. It is an irritant and may be indicative of other problems, such as the death of the shareholder or that he has moved without notifying the company. The absolute minimum should probably be a letter of enquiry but further steps may well be considered if necessary, especially if the amount is large.

The company's obligations will partly depend on its articles. Reg. 108 of Table A states:

> 'Any dividend which has remained unclaimed for twelve years from the date when it became due for payment shall, if the directors so resolve, be forfeited and cease to remain owing by the company.'

Unclaimed dividends are statute-barred after 12 years in England and Wales and five years in Scotland, though case law is slightly ambiguous. The periods run from the date that the due payment is last acknowledged.

302 Do the owners of partly paid shares rank for the payment of a full dividend?

It depends on the articles. Reg. 104 of Table A provides that dividends shall be paid according to the amount paid up. So if Mr A has fully paid up his one pound share and Mr B has only paid 50p of his one pound share, Mr A's dividend will be twice the size of Mr B's dividend. Furthermore, Reg. 104 also provides that payment shall be pro-rata to the time during the period in which the money had been received by the company, but if any share is issued on terms providing that it shall rank for dividend as from a particular date, that share shall rank for dividend accordingly. As so often is the case, it is necessary to look at the articles.

seven

Listed companies and corporate governance 303-324

seven
Listed companies and corporate governance

Listed companies

303 What is UKLA and who is responsible for it?

UKLA stands for UK Listing Authority and it is the responsibility of the Financial Services Authority. UKLA is empowered to make rules governing admission to listing, the continuing obligations of issues, the enforcement of the obligations and suspension and cancellation of listing.

304 Can UKLA impose financial penalties?

Yes, it can impose financial penalties on listed companies. It can also impose financial penalties on the directors of listed companies if they knowingly contravene the listing rules.

305 What is the status of AIM?

AIM stands for the Alternative Investment Market. It is run by the London Stock Exchange and it is intended as a market for smaller companies. AIM companies are not subject to the Listing Rules and are not listed for the purposes of statutory or regulatory requirements. They are subject to separate AIM rules issued by the London Stock Exchange.

306 What are OFEX and Nasdaq Europe?

OFEX is regulated by the Financial Services Authority and is a prescribed market for the purposes of section 118 of the Financial Services and Markets Act. The entry requirements for OFEX are not as demanding as those for the Official List or for AIM. Companies quoted on OFEX must comply with the obligations set out in the OFEX rule book.

Nasdaq Europe is a wholly owned subsidiary of Nasdaq, the American market that specialises in high technology companies. Nasdaq Europe is based in London and Brussels.

307 How many quoted companies are there?

There are about 1,290 fully listed companies, though obviously the number varies from time to time. This number does not include companies quoted on AIM or OFEX.

308 What is the SETS system of trading?

It is an automated order-driven system for dealing in about 200 UK equities, including the FTSE 100 companies.

Corporate governance

309 How have corporate governance codes developed since 1992?

Corporate governance has developed since 1992 with the publication of the following codes:

1992 Cadbury Code

This was a code of best practice in corporate governance. It was issued by a committee convened by the Financial Reporting Council and chaired by Sir Adrian Cadbury.

1995 Greenbury Code

This was a report on various aspects of directors' remuneration. The committee was established by the CBI and chaired by Sir Richard Greenbury.

1998 The Hampel Combined Code

This was the report of a committee established by the Financial Reporting Council and chaired by Sir Ronald Hampel. It reviewed the operation of the Cadbury and Greenbury codes, brought them together (hence the Combined Code), amended them and added its own contribution.

2003 The Combined Code on Corporate Governance

This followed a review by Derek Higgs and brought the Combined Code up to date. It has been adopted for financial periods commencing on or after 1st November 2003.

310 Does the Combined Code apply to all companies?

No, it does not. It applies to listed companies and is annexed to the listing rules. Changes to the listing rules have been made because of it. Of course it is of interest to other companies and may influence their governance.

311 Are smaller listed companies exempted from some of the requirements of the Combined Code?

Yes, they are. Companies that were not in the FTSE 350 throughout the year immediately before the reporting year may:

- Have just two independent non-executive directors. This is instead of half the board, excluding the chairman.

- Have remuneration and audit committees comprising two independent non-executive directors. This is instead of three.

312 Does the Combined Code have the force of law behind it?

No, it does not. It is compulsory for listed companies to the extent that they are required to comply on a point by point basis or explain on a point by point basis why they have not complied. Not to do so would incur the wrath of the Financial Services Authority.

313 How is the Combined Code laid out?

The code is divided into a number of subject areas. For each one there is a main principle, supporting principles and code provisions.

314 What are the subject areas covered by the Combined Code?

They are:

Directors

- The Board
- Chairman and chief executive
- Board balance and independence
- Appointments to the board
- Information and professional development
- Performance evaluation

Remuneration

- The level and make-up of remuneration
- Procedure

Accountability and Audit

- Financial reporting
- Internal control
- Audit committee and auditors

Relations with Shareholders

- Dialogue with institutional shareholders

- Constructive use of the AGM

Institutional Shareholders

- Dialogue with companies

- Evaluation of governance disclosures

- Shareholder voting

315 How must a listed company disclose how it has complied with the Combined Code?

Listed companies are required to make a disclosure statement in two parts. The first part must show how it has applied both the main and supporting principles. The second part must confirm whether or not it has complied with the detailed code provisions and to the extent that it has not, its reasons for not doing so. This second part is sometimes known as 'comply or explain'.

316 What exactly is meant by comply or explain?

Fears are sometimes expressed that corporate governance could turn into a box ticking exercise, and that companies could be required to blindly follow rules that may not be suitable for their particular circumstances. Almost everyone thinks that, were it to happen, it would be a great pity. This is why the Combined Code is formulated on the basis of comply or explain. Companies may depart from the provisions of the code, but they must disclose that they have done so and give their reasons. It is then up to investors and others to judge whether the reasons are good ones, and act accordingly if they think that they are not.

317 I invest in a company that does not comply with all the detailed provisions of the Combined Code. Am I right to be desperately worried?

Not necessarily so, and the fact that you are will concern many people who feel that corporate governance is turning into a box ticking exercise. What you should do is study the company's explanation, which you will see, and use your judgement about whether it is a good one. If you think that it is not, you will be right to be worried.

318 I have looked at the Combined Code and some of its provisions seem bland and obvious. Do others think this?

Yes, they do, though of course it is not all like that. As an example of what you mean, how about *'All directors must take decisions objectively and in the interests of the company'*. Does this really need saying and is there anyone who would disagree?

319 What does the Combined Code say about combining the role of chairman and chief executive?

This is one of the most controversial topics and you may be able to think of some outstanding individuals who have combined the roles very success-fully. On the other hand, you can probably think of instances where it has been a disaster. Most people think that it is dangerous and not a good idea, and the Code takes this view. It states:

> *'The roles of chairman and chief executive should not be exercised by the same individual. The division of responsibilities between the chairman and chief executive should be clearly established, set out in writing and agreed by the board.'*

320 What does the Combined Code say about the balance on the board between executive and non-executive directors?

The Code states that there should be a balance of executive and non-exec-utive directors (and in particular of independent non-executive directors) so that no individual or small group of individuals, can dominate the board's decision taking. Except for smaller companies, at least half the board, excluding the chairman, should comprise non-executives determined by the board to be independent.

321 How does the Combined Code define an independent non-executive director?

It does not give a definitive definition but it does say:

> 'The board should state its reasons if it determines that a director is independent notwithstanding the existence of relationships or circumstances which may appear relevant to its determination, including if the director:
>
> - has been an employee of the company or group within the last five years;
>
> - has, or has had within the last three years, a material business relationship with the company either directly, or as a partner, shareholder, director or senior employee of a body that has such a relationship with the company;
>
> - has received or receives additional remuneration from the company apart from a director's fee, participates in the company's share option or a performance-related pay scheme, or is a member of the company's pension scheme;
>
> - has close family ties with any of the company's advisors, directors or senior employees;
>
> - holds cross-directorships or has significant links with other directors through involvement in other companies or bodies;
>
> - represents a significant shareholder; or
>
> - has served on the board for more than nine years from the date of their first election.'

322 Does the Combined Code allow directors to have lengthy periods of notice?

It depends whether or not you consider a year to be a lengthy period. The Code states:

> 'Notice or contract periods should be set at one year or less. If it is necessary to offer longer notice or contract periods to new directors recruited from outside, such periods should reduce to one year or less after the initial period.'

Not too long ago a notice period of up to five years was not unusual.

323 What does the Combined Code say about directors' remuneration?

It says quite a lot including the following:

> 'Levels of remuneration should be sufficient to attract, retain and motivate directors of the quality required to run the company successfully, but a company should avoid paying more than is necessary for this purpose. A significant proportion of executive directors' remuneration should be structured so as to link rewards to corporate and individual performance.'

> 'The remuneration committee should judge where to position their company relative to other companies. But they should use such comparisons with caution, in view of the risk of an upward ratchet of remuneration levels with no corresponding improvement in performance. They should also be sensitive to pay and employment conditions elsewhere in the group, especially when determining annual salary increases.'

> 'The performance-related elements of remuneration should form a significant proportion of the total remuneration package of executive directors and should be designed to align their interests with those of shareholders and to give these directors keen incentives to perform at the highest levels.'

'Levels of remuneration for non-executive directors should reflect the time commitment and responsibilities of the role. Remuneration for non-executive directors should not include share options. If, exceptionally, options are granted, shareholder approval should be sought in advance and any shares acquired by exercise of the options should be held until at least one year after the non-executive director leaves the board.'

It should be remembered that the Combined Code is for listed companies. It applies on a 'comply or explain' basis.

324 The guidance in the Combined Code seems sensible but somehow directors' remuneration in listed companies goes up year after year. Why is this and is it 'fat cattery'?

You are not the only person too have noticed the phenomenon. Every year for many years, in good times and bad, directors' remuneration in listed companies, on average, rises faster than general inflation and faster than wages generally. There are companies and directors that buck the trend, but the general rule holds. It cannot go on for ever and in recent years investors have shown signs of restiveness. They now get an advisory vote on the directors' remuneration report at the annual general meeting.

Perhaps a clue to a possible reason lies in the second quotation from the Combined Code given in the previous answer. Directors frequently choose to position their remuneration in the upper quartile, or at or above average. It is a statistical impossibility for almost everyone to be paid above average, so these policies inevitably ratchet up the remuneration. Is it fat cattery? To coin a phrase "You can say that, but I could not possibly comment".

eight

The elective regime, resolutions and notice 325-361

eight
The elective regime, resolutions and notice

The elective regime

325 What is the elective regime?

The elective regime is an option for all private companies, including private companies that are subsidiaries of public companies. It is not available to public companies. The elective regime was made available by the 1989 Companies Act and it is a significant step towards deregulation for private companies. Each of the individual elective measures is an option for the members of a private company. None of them are compulsory and the members may adopt all the measures or any combination of them.

326 What are the elective measures?

The five available elective measures are:

1.   The period for which a general meeting may authorise the directors to allot shares may be extended beyond the normal five years. A longer period may be substituted or the period may be made indefinite.

2.   Accounts and reports need not be laid before the members in a general meeting.

3.   Annual general meetings need not be held.

4.   The percentage of shares required to be held by persons agreeing to an extraordinary general meeting being held (or to a resolution being passed as a special resolution) on short notice, may be reduced from 95 per cent of the class down to not less than 90 per cent.

5.   Auditors need not be appointed annually.

If an elective resolution is passed not to lay accounts and reports before a general meeting, they must still be sent to the members. The measures most commonly adopted are not holding annual general meetings and not laying the accounts before the members in a meeting.

327 Is the elective regime likely to be relevant to my company?

It may well be helpful, especially the possibility of not holding annual general meetings and not laying the accounts before members in a meeting. The great majority of private companies only have a few members and they may feel that they can dispense with a certain amount of formality and bureaucracy. In many cases the members are related or feel that they can place a great deal of trust in each other. The elective regime is of course useful when there is a single member, including the situation where the single member is a holding company.

In practice the elective regime is unlikely to help when there are a lot of members. This is because it will be very difficult to obtain 100 per cent support from those entitled to vote. A single abstention blocks it. Arguably it may be less suitable when there are a lot of members.

328 How do the members pass an elective resolution, and how and when does it cease to have effect?

21 clear days notice must be given of an elective resolution and the notice must state that it is to be proposed as an elective resolution. An elective resolution must receive the support of everyone entitled to attend and vote. A single person voting against or abstaining will prevent it being passed.

An elective resolution stays in effect indefinitely or until it is cancelled. It does not need periodic renewal. A resolution to cancel an elective resolution may be passed as an ordinary resolution. It also ceases to have effect if the company becomes a public company.

329 I am not in favour of the elective regime for my company. Can I block it?

If you are a voting member and if an elective resolution has not yet been passed, you have a veto. This is because the resolution must be passed unanimously and will be blocked by a single abstention or vote against. If an elective resolution is already in force, a simple majority is required to cancel it. All this is a matter for decision by the members. The directors can make recommendations and put resolutions to meetings, but the members decide.

If you object to not holding annual general meetings or not laying the accounts and reports before the company in a meeting, you still have an effective veto even after the resolution has been passed. This is because any single member can require them to happen in any particular year and the same member can require it year after year. The auditor can also require the accounts to be laid before the company in a particular year.

330 I have heard that the elective regime will be the norm for all private companies and perhaps even made compulsory. Is this correct?

It is correct that the elective regime will probably become the norm for private companies, but it is almost certainly wrong to think that it will be compulsory. The Company Law Review Steering Group recommended that all the elective measures should automatically apply to newly formed private companies, unless the founder members wrote into the company's constitution that any or all of them were not wanted. It also recommended that it should be easier to pass elective resolutions in existing companies, and harder to cancel elective measures in place in existing companies. All this is Government policy and likely to be enacted in the next main Companies Act. The Government has no intention of making the elective measures compulsory for any company.

331 Does the elective regime make it impossible to pay a dividend?

No, it does not do this. Table A and most company articles allow the directors to declare and pay one or more interim dividends. A final dividend may only be paid up to the maximum amount proposed by the directors, and must be approved by the members. The solution is to pay all dividends as interim dividends declared by the directors, and never pay a final dividend. Alternative solutions are for the members to declare a final dividend by means of a unanimous written resolution or to hold an extraordinary general meeting at which the members can declare a final dividend.

332 How do we appoint the auditors when the elective regime applies?

The Act requires that the auditors be appointed or re-appointed annually, and that the directors may appoint the first auditors or fill a casual vacancy. However, if the elective regime is in force, the auditors continue to act until they resign or are removed. If the auditors resign whilst the elective regime is in force, the directors may fill the vacancy and appoint new auditors.

333 How do we overcome the problem of directors retiring by rotation?

Table A provides that all directors retire at the company's first annual general meeting and that one third of the directors retire at each subsequent annual general meeting. Retiring directors can of course offer themselves for re-election. Many articles contain similar provisions. There is an obvious conflict if an elective resolution is in force and annual general meetings are not held. The solution is a special resolution to change the articles so that directors do not retire, but serve until they die, resign, become ineligible or are removed.

Resolutions

334 What determines what type of resolution is required for a vote by the members?

The Act and the Insolvency Act require that certain items of business must be the subject of certain types of resolution and this may also be stipulated by the articles. However, articles may not stipulate a less rigorous requirement than the Act, and if they do, the Act takes precedence and will prevail. If neither the Act nor the articles specify a particular type of resolution, it will be the subject of an ordinary resolution.

335 How is a special resolution passed?

A special resolution must be passed with a majority of at least 75 per cent of those voting. Votes not cast are disregarded for this purpose. So if 100 votes may be cast, 60 are cast in favour, 20 are cast against and 20 are not cast, a special resolution will be carried. 21 clear days notice must be given of a special resolution, and this is so whether it is to be proposed at an annual general meeting or at an extraordinary general meeting. The notice must give the exact wording of the resolution and must state that it is to be proposed as a special resolution.

336 What types of business must be the subject of special resolutions?

The Act and the Insolvency Act provide quite a long list including the following:

- Altering the articles.
- Altering the objects clause in the memorandum or conditions in the memorandum which could have been in the articles of association.
- Changing the company's name.
- Disapplying members' statutory pre-emption rights.
- Approving, where permissible, the provision of financial assistance for the purpose of shares or agreements for the purchase of its own shares by a private company.

- Reducing capital.

- Procuring the winding up of the company by the court.

- Voluntarily winding up a solvent company.

Company articles may specify that certain types of business must be the subject of special resolutions.

337 How is an extraordinary resolution passed?

An extraordinary resolution must be passed with a majority of at least 75 per cent of those voting. Votes not cast are disregarded for this purpose. So if 100 votes may be cast, 60 are cast in favour, 20 are cast against and 20 are not cast, an extraordinary resolution will be carried. 21 clear days notice must be given of an extraordinary resolution to be proposed at an annual general meeting. 14 clear days notice must be given of an extraordinary resolution to be proposed at an extraordinary general meeting.

You may notice that the requirements are very similar to the requirements for a special resolution. The only difference is that only 14 days notice need be given if an extraordinary resolution is to be proposed at an extraordinary general meeting.

338 What types of business must be the subject of extraordinary resolutions?

There are not many actions that require an extraordinary resolution. They include:

- To vary the rights of a class of shares.

- In the case of a voluntary winding up, to sanction the use of certain powers by a liquidator.

- To voluntarily wind up the company on the grounds that it cannot meet its liabilities.

Company articles may specify that certain types of business must be the subject of extraordinary resolutions.

339 What is an ordinary resolution and when is one needed?

An ordinary resolution is passed by a simple majority of those voting, disregarding those entitled to vote but who do not do so. So if 300 are present, with each person having one vote, 62 vote in favour and 61 vote against, an ordinary resolution will be carried. All resolutions are ordinary resolutions unless the Act or company articles specify otherwise.

There are two events where the Act specifies the requirement for an ordinary resolution and this takes precedence over anything to the contrary in the articles. They are a resolution to remove a director before the expiry of his term of office and a resolution to remove an auditor before the expiry of his term of office.

340 When is special notice of an ordinary resolution required and what are the procedures?

Certain types of business require special notice to be given. When this has been done the resolution is decided by a simple majority of those voting.

Special notice must be given to the company at least 28 days before the meeting at which the resolution is to be proposed. This may be done by a member or members holding 10 per cent of the voting rights. The company must then give notice to the members of the resolution. This is normally done with the notice of the meeting. However, it may be done separately so long as members receive 21 clear days notice. In practice, it is often done for items for a forthcoming annual general meeting. Of course it is often the directors who give special notice.

Special notice is required for the following matters:

- To remove an auditor before his period of office has expired, and also to appoint a new auditor before the expiry of the period of office of an auditor, to re-appoint an auditor who was appointed by the directors to fill a casual vacancy, or to fill a casual vacancy in the position of auditor.

- To remove a director before the expiry of his period of office.

- To appoint (or reappoint) a director who is over the age limit. This applies only to public companies and to private companies that are subsidiaries of public companies.

341 How is an elective resolution passed and how is a resolution to cancel an elective resolution passed?

Elective resolutions are available to all private companies, including private companies that are subsidiaries of public companies. They are a step towards deregulation and the purposes for which they are available are detailed in the answer to the next question.

21 clear days notice must be given of an elective resolution and the notice must state that it is to be proposed as an elective resolution. An elective resolution must receive the support of everyone entitled to attend and vote. A single person voting against or abstaining will prevent it being passed.

A resolution to cancel an elective resolution may be passed as an ordinary resolution. It also ceases to have effect if the company becomes a public company.

342 What types of business may be the subject of elective resolutions?

Elective resolutions may be proposed to do one or more of the following:

- To remove or extend the duration of authority to allot shares.
- To dispense with the laying of accounts and reports before the general meeting.
- To dispense with the holding of annual general meetings.
- To reduce the majority required to authorise short notice of a meeting.
- To dispense with the appointment of auditors annually.

343 Can a resolution of the members be passed as a written resolution?

It can in a private company and the convenience of a written resolution has obvious attractions. It saves holding a meeting and it saves waiting during the period of notice.

To be effective a written resolution must have the unanimous support of everyone entitled to attend and vote, so one member opposing the resolution or abstaining makes it impossible and so does a member who cannot be contacted. For this reason it is usually only of practical use if the company has relatively few members. The signatures may be on a single piece of paper or several pieces of paper, and it takes effect as soon as the last piece of paper is delivered to the company. A director who has knowledge of a proposed written resolution is required to notify the auditors.

A written resolution may not be used to remove a directors or auditors before the expiry of their terms of office. This is because it would deprive them of their rights to state their cases. Any other resolution of members in a private company may be passed as a written resolution. This includes special, extraordinary and elective resolutions. If a resolution must be registered with the Registrar of Companies, it must be registered if it is in the form of a written resolution.

344 I have heard that a decision may be taken as an informal corporate act rather than by passing a resolution. How does this happen?

You have heard correctly. Judges have long taken the view, and not just in company matters, that if a group of men and women are absolutely unanimous, it is unnecessary to insist on the formalities of their constitution. This common law doctrine is recognised by the Act.

The members can take most decisions as an informal corporate act, provided that they are absolutely unanimous. There is no notice, no resolution and no meeting – the members just act. There are though, just a few decisions that cannot be made in this way, and they include the removal of a director or an auditor, but most decisions that would normally require a special, extraordinary or elective resolution may be taken as an informal corporate act.

There is a rather optimistic requirement that informal corporate acts be minuted as though decisions had been taken at a meeting. Also they must where applicable be registered with the Registrar of Companies as though they had been taken as resolutions in a meeting. Furthermore, it will probably not escape your notice that in the event of a challenge it may be difficult to show that there was 100 per cent agreement to an informal corporate act.

345 Would you please summarise the required notice periods for the different resolutions and also the majority of votes cast in each?

	Notice Period	Approval Necessary
Special resolution	21 clear days	75 per cent
Extraordinary resolution	21 clear days at AGM 14 clear days at EGM	75 per cent
Ordinary resolution	–	50 per cent plus 1
Ordinary resolution with special notice	21 clear days	50 per cent plus 1
Elective resolution	21 clear days	100 per cent of those entitled to attend and vote
Resolution to cancel an elective resolution	21 clear days	50 per cent plus 1
Written resolution	–	100 per cent of those entitled to attend and vote

346 Would you please explain what is meant by 'clear days'?

In England and Wales the day that the notice is posted must be added and so must the day of the meeting. Also 48 hours must be added for the post. If there is a Saturday, Sunday or bank holiday in the 48 hour posting period, these must be added too. The effect of this is that, for example, 21 clear days always means at least 25 calendar days. If the notices were to be posted on Friday 23rd December, 21 clear days would mean 28 calendar days. In Scotland 'clear days' are always one day less than in England and Wales. This is because the day of the meeting is not included.

The concept of 'clear days' applies to notice periods for meetings as well as notice of resolutions.

347 What resolutions of members must be registered with the Registrar of Companies?

These are listed in section 380 of the Act and are:

- Special resolutions.

- Extraordinary resolutions.

- Elective resolutions and resolutions to cancel elective resolutions.

- Resolutions of, or binding members of, a class of shareholders.

- Resolutions passed by the directors in order to effect a change of company name on the direction of the Secretary of State under section 31 (2).

- Resolutions to give, vary, revoke or renew an authority to the directors for the allotment of certain securities under section 80.

- A resolution of the directors to alter the company memorandum on the company ceasing to be a public company under section 147 (2).

- A resolution conferring, varying, revoking, or renewing authority for a market purchase by the company of its own shares under section 166.

- A resolution for voluntary winding up under section 84 (1) (a) of the Insolvency Act.

- A resolution of the directors of an old public company that the company should be re-registered as a public company under section 2 (1) of the Consequential Provisions Act.

NOTICE

General

348 Who has the authority to issue a notice convening a meeting of members?

Nearly all meetings of companies are convened by the directors. This should be a board decision and not a decision taken by one or more directors. Directors are compelled to convene an extraordinary general meeting if a valid requisition is received from the necessary number of members. In certain unusual circumstances a meeting may be convened by some of the members, on the instructions of the Department of Trade and Industry or on the instructions of the court. Reg. 37 of Table A provides that if there are not within the United Kingdom sufficient directors to call a general meeting, any director or any member of the company may do so.

The notice convening the meeting must state the authority of the signatory. It is usual for notices to be signed by the secretary following the words *'By Order of the Board'*.

349 To whom should notices be sent?

The list is:

a)   *All members* – this is subject to any limitations in the articles. Each joint member should receive a notice unless, which is usually the case, the articles provide otherwise.

b)   *Directors* – this depends on the articles but it is usually the case.

c)   *Auditors* – this is a statutory requirement.

These are the standard requirements but the requirement may extend to others in certain cases and where special requirements are imposed by the articles. Preference shareholders may be a case in point.

350 What is the consequence if a notice is not sent to someone entitled to receive a notice?

The meeting may be challenged and business conducted at it may be declared to be invalid.

351 What is the position if there is an innocent error in sending out the notices?

It depends on the articles but companies usually have an article consistent with Reg. 39 of Table A, which states:

> 'The accidental omission to give notice of a meeting to or the non-receipt of notice of a meeting by, any person entitled to receive notice shall not invalidate the proceedings at that meeting.'

This is just as well as the largest companies have a million or more shareholders. It would otherwise be exceedingly unfortunate if 999,999 notices were safely posted and one fell down a crack in the floorboards.

The words *'accidental omission'* should be particularly noticed. A deliberate omission may well invalidate the meeting, even if the deliberate omission was for a presumed good reason. For example, a failure to send a notice to a member who was believed to be away (and actually was away) has been held to be not an accidental omission, with the result that the meeting was held to be invalid.

352 What are the requirements for notice to be given of an adjourned meeting?

When a meeting is adjourned to a fixed date, notice is not necessary unless the articles provide differently. This is because business that may be conducted at the adjourned meeting is limited to business that could have been conducted at the original meeting. If, however, different business is to be conducted, what amounts to a new meeting is held and new notice of sufficient length must be given. Reg. 45 of Table A specifies that, if an adjournment is for 14 days or more, notice of at least seven clear days must be given.

353 Is the notice that convenes a meeting relevant to establishing whether or not it is an annual general meeting?

It is, and what is more it is the determining factor. A notice should say whether the meeting is an annual general meeting or an extraordinary general meeting. A meeting is only an annual general meeting if this is stated by the notice that convened it. If the notice is silent on the point, the meeting is automatically an extraordinary general meeting.

Notice periods

354 What are the required periods of notice for the different types of meeting?

The minimum periods specified by the Act are:

- 21 clear days for an annual general meeting.

- 14 days for an extraordinary general meeting of a limited company.

- 7 clear days for an extraordinary general meeting of an unlimited company.

'Clear days' were defined in the answer to Question 346. If the articles specify longer periods than the above, they will apply. If the articles specify shorter periods than the above, the particular articles, except in respect of an adjourned meeting, will be void and the above periods will apply.

Certain types of resolution require certain periods of notice. If they are longer than the periods given above, then longer notice must be given. For example, 21 clear days notice of a special resolution to be proposed at an extraordinary general meeting of a limited company must be given.

355 In what circumstances is short notice possible?

Short notice of an annual general meeting is only possible with the consent of 100 per cent of those entitled to attend and vote.

Short notice of an extraordinary general meeting is possible if **both** the following are satisfied:

- there is the consent of the majority of those entitled to attend and vote; **and**

- there is the consent of members holding 95 per cent of the voting rights at the meeting.

In a private company having a relevant elective resolution in force, the proportion of 95 per cent mentioned above may be reduced to 90 per cent or a proportion between 90 per cent and 95 per cent. You should note that short notice is not the same as no notice.

356 Would you please give an example of how short notice works?

Let us assume that a company has 11 shareholders and that one of them has 95 per cent of the votes. In order to approve short notice of an extraordinary general meeting it would be necessary to have the support of six shareholders including the one holding 95 per cent. Short notice of an annual general meeting would not be possible unless every shareholder consents.

Content of notices

357 What must be included in a notice convening a meeting?

A notice should contain:

- The date and time of the meeting.
- The place of the meeting.
- Whether the meeting is an annual general meeting or an extraordinary general meeting.
- A general description of the business to be transacted.
- The precise wording of certain resolutions.

If the members have the right to appoint a proxy or proxies to attend and vote on their behalf, which is the case in all companies having a share capital, the notice must contain or be accompanied by a statement of the members' rights in this matter.

358 Are there any particular requirements concerning the date, place and time of a meeting?

The choice is made by the persons who convene the meeting, which is almost always the directors. They have a common law duty to make the date, place and time reasonably convenient for the majority of members. Failure to do this could lead to a successful challenge. To take an extreme and fanciful example, 11.30 pm on Christmas Eve at the top of Mount Snowdon would undoubtedly be deemed to be not reasonably convenient for the majority of members.

359 What exactly is meant by the requirement that a notice should give a general description of the business to be transacted?

Members must be given sufficient information for them to make an informed choice about whether or not they wish to attend and vote at the meeting. If they do not receive the required standard of information, there is a risk that business transacted may be held to be invalid. Fuller details must be given of any business that the articles fix as special business and the precise wording of certain resolutions must be given. Over and above this the notice must make it clear, in general terms, what business is to be conducted. This may seem rather imprecise but it is the explanation usually given.

360 What is the minimum information about proxies that must be included in a notice?

Every notice of a meeting of a company having a share capital whether public or private, must include or be accompanied by a statement to the effect that a member entitled to attend and vote is entitled to appoint a proxy (or proxies in the case of a public company) to attend and vote on his behalf, and that such proxy need not himself be a member of the company.

361 Is it essential that proxy forms accompany notices?

Except for listed companies, and subject to anything to the contrary in the articles, there is no compulsion to circulate proxy forms with the notices. It is, though, often done.

nine

Meetings 362-430

nine

Meetings

MEMBERS' MEETINGS

General

362 Can the members insist that an extraordinary general meeting be held?

A member or members of a company with a share capital holding not less than one-tenth of the paid-up capital carrying voting rights, may at any time lodge a requisition requiring the directors to convene an extraordinary general meeting for the purposes stated in the requisition. If the company does not have a share capital, members holding not less than one-tenth of the voting rights may do it. Anything in the articles that purports to make it more difficult or impossible is overruled by the Act. Articles can, however, make it easier for members to requisition a meeting.

363 Who has the right to attend a members' meeting?

Subject to the articles it is members attending in person, duly appointed proxies of members, duly appointed representatives of corporate members, the directors and the auditor. Other people, such as members' advisers, may attend with the consent of the meeting, but the consent may be withheld or withdrawn at any time for any reason. If this happens, the people affected must leave the meeting.

364 Is it possible to amend special, extraordinary or elective resolutions, resolutions to cancel elective resolutions and ordinary resolutions requiring special notice?

No, it is not possible. This is because members must have notice of the precise wording. If an amendment is allowed, they do not have notice of the precise wording.

365 Is it necessary to give notice of an adjourned meeting?

It depends on the articles. Table A says that notice of at least seven clear days must be given if the meeting is adjourned for fourteen days or more, and that the notice must give details of the time, place and general nature of the business. If the adjournment is for less than fourteen days, notice is not necessary.

366 What business can be conducted at an adjourned meeting?

Table A states that no business can be conducted at an adjourned meeting that could not have been conducted at the original meeting. This means that it must be within the terms of the notice that convened the original meeting.

367 What rights does a proxy have at a members' meeting?

At a meeting of a private company a proxy has the same right to speak as the member that he represents. At a meeting of a public company this is not the case and a proxy may only speak with the consent of the chairman. Unless the articles provide otherwise, a proxy may count towards a quorum but may not vote on a show of hands. Table A does not provide otherwise. A proxy may join in a demand for a poll and may vote on a poll.

368 My company has 100 shares registered in joint names and the joint shareholders disagree about how the votes should be cast. Does each shareholder cast 50 votes as they wish?

Not if Table A applies, though your articles might allow it. Table A allows the first named in the register of members to cast the votes on all 100 shares.

369 Can votes be cast by a citizen of a country with which we are at war?

The right of an enemy alien to vote personally or by proxy is suspended in time of war. Whether or not a state of war exists is often no longer the clear-cut decision that was formerly the case. On 3rd September 1939 Mr Neville Chamberlain said "I have to tell you that no such assurance has been received and that consequently this country is at war with Germany". On the other hand, in 1956 during the Suez crisis Sir Anthony Eden said "This is not a war – it is a state of armed conflict". Since then the distinction seems to have got even more blurred.

Quorum

370 What is the quorum for a members' meeting?

It depends on the articles. Table A states:

> 'No business shall be transacted at any meeting unless a quorum is present. Two persons entitled to vote upon the business to be transacted, each being a member or a proxy for a member or a duly authorised representative of a corporation, shall be a quorum.'

If the number of members is less than the number for a quorum fixed by the articles, the presence of every member will constitute a quorum. In a single-member company the presence of the single member will constitute a quorum.

371 What happens if a quorum is not present or if a quorum ceases to be present?

It depends on the articles. Table A states:

> 'If such a quorum is not present within half an hour from the time appointed for the meeting, or if during a meeting such a quorum ceases to be present, the meeting shall stand adjourned to the same day in the next week at the same time and place or to such time and place as the directors may determine.'

372 What happens if it is not possible to obtain a quorum?

This can happen if the number for a quorum is set unrealistically high or if the number of members falls to or close to, the number required for a quorum. It can also happen if one or more members stay away from meetings in a deliberate attempt to frustrate the business of the company, or to prevent a vote that they think would reach a decision contrary to their wishes.

If it is not possible to obtain a quorum, any director or any member entitled to vote can apply to the court for an order. The court can, if it sees fit, order that a meeting be held and it can stipulate such rules as it sees fit for the meeting. The court can, if it sees fit, order that the articles be overruled for this one meeting and that a single member shall constitute a quorum. The meeting can conduct necessary business and can, if the members so decide, pass a special resolution to change the articles so that for future meetings a lower number shall constitute a quorum. This has been done many times.

Annual general meeting

373 Must a company hold annual general meetings and, if so, what are the laws concerning timing?

A private company that has passed an appropriate elective resolution need not hold annual general meetings. Otherwise the requirements are as follows:

- The first annual general meeting must be held within 18 months of incorporation. Subject to this it is not necessary to hold an AGM in the calendar year of incorporation or in the following calendar year.

- Annual general meetings must not be more than 15 months apart.

- One, and only one, annual general meeting must be held in each calendar year.

A company must comply with both the second and third points. It is not sufficient to hold a meeting in December, then hold one 14 months later in January.

A meeting is the annual general meeting if this is the description used in the notice that calls it; otherwise it is not.

374 We are getting close to the last permitted date for the annual general meeting and the accounts are not ready. What can we do?

You could try harder to get the accounts ready, but you have probably already thought of that. There are two possibilities:

- You could hold the annual general meeting without laying the accounts, then lay the accounts later at an extraordinary general meeting. Accounts are normally laid at an AGM, but subject to anything to the contrary in the articles it is permitted to lay them at an extraordinary general meeting.

- The AGM could be opened then adjourned to a later date when the accounts will be ready. This does comply with the law but of course it can only be done with the consent of the members.

375 Must certain business be conducted at an AGM and is there some business that cannot be conducted at an AGM?

Subject to anything to the contrary in the articles, the answer is no to both questions. All business can be conducted at an AGM and all business can be conducted at an EGM. Certain business is normally conducted at an AGM but this is a matter of convention, and possibly also of convenience and expense.

376 What is the normal business of an annual general meeting?

The usual business of an annual general meeting is:

- Consideration of the accounts and reports.

- Declaration of a final dividend, if one is to be paid.

- Appointment or reappointment of the auditors and the fixing of their remuneration. In practice it is usually resolved that their remuneration be fixed by the directors.

- The election or re-election of directors.

All these matters are the subject of ordinary resolutions.

377 Is it lawful to hold an annual general meeting at which no business is transacted?

Yes, with the consent of the members. Such a meeting can count as the annual general meeting for the year.

378 Can the members require that a resolution be circulated in connection with a forthcoming annual general meeting?

A requisition may be given by the holders of not less than 5 per cent of the total voting rights exercisable at the meeting to which the requisition relates. Alternatively it may be given by at least 100 members holding shares in the company on which there has been paid up an average sum, per member, of not less than £100.

The requisitions can require notice to be given of a resolution that it is intended to be moved at the next annual general meeting. They can also require that a statement up to 1,000 words long be circulated. The expense of doing this will fall on the requisitionists unless the meeting decides otherwise.

Chairman and conduct of meetings

379 Who will be the chairman of a members' meeting?

It depends on the articles. Table A says that it will be the chairman of the board of directors, if any, if present and willing to act. If this situation does not obtain, it will be any director nominated by the board of directors, if present and willing to act. If, 15 minutes after the time appointed for the start of the meeting, no director is present and willing to act, the members present may choose one of their number to act as chairman.

380 Does the chairman have a casting vote?

The chairman has no inherent right to a casting vote and only has one if it is given by the articles. This is usually the case and Table A does give the chairman a casting vote in addition to any other vote that he might have.

381 Must the chairman's casting vote be exercised in a particular way?

You may be thinking of the convention (but not the law) by which the Speaker of the House of Commons uses his casting vote to leave the matter open. So, for example, in the event of a tie on a motion of confidence in Her Majesty's Government, the Speaker votes with the Government to defeat the motion. In 1979 James Callaghan's Government lost a motion of confidence by just one vote and then lost the subsequent general election. Had the Government received just one more vote the Speaker's casting vote would have kept it in office. You may think that this has little relevance to company directors and company secretaries, and you would be quite right, but it is very interesting. There is no such law or convention for company meetings. The chairman can use his casting vote as he sees fit in the interests of the company as a whole as he in good faith sees it. Whatever he does he will displease half the company. It makes no difference if he has had one or more votes in the tied vote.

382 From what does the chairman derive his powers?

The chairman derives his powers from the meeting. A group of people want him to act as chairman and control the meeting on their behalf, or at least they are members of a company whose articles provide that he will be the chairman and act for them. Statutory law is a factor in a few cases and the articles will be relevant. In many cases common law decisions set limits to, and guidance for, the authority of the chairman.

383 What are the duties of the chairman?

The chairman should preserve order and do his best to ensure that the meeting is fairly and properly conducted. He should ensure that all shades of opinion have a fair hearing. His primary duty is to assist the members to ascertain the sense of the meeting and reach decisions. A key part of this is the fair and efficient general running of the meeting and, in particular, the taking of votes and declaring the results.

The articles may lay down certain responsibilities and any provisions in the articles should be observed. Table A gives the following rights and responsibilities to the chairman:

- To declare conclusively, and without proof of the number of votes, the result of a vote on a show of hands.

- To demand a poll and to insist that a poll be taken after a valid demand has been withdrawn.

- To direct where and how a poll shall be taken.

- To exercise a casting vote.

- To rule on the validity of votes tendered at the meeting.

384 Must the chairman allow everyone to speak, to say exactly what they want and to take as long as they wish?

No, no and no respectively. To take the points one by one:

1) It is obviously impractical in some meetings to let everyone speak, as the number present may be very large. The chairman should allow all points of view a reasonable hearing. If the number present is small, it might be reasonable to allow everyone to speak who wishes to do so.

2) The chairman should encourage speakers to keep to the issue under consideration, though this may be a matter of opinion and interpretation. He should not allow personal abuse and offensive behaviour, though this too can be a matter of opinion and interpretation.

3) It is usually reasonable to ask speakers to limit their remarks to a certain length. Care should be taken that any restrictions are reasonable and that all points of view are treated in the same way.

385 What are the chairman's powers to adjourn the meeting?

Unless the articles give the chairman power to adjourn, which Table A does not, he may only adjourn with the consent of the meeting or on the instructions of the meeting. If he tries to adjourn without the consent of the meeting, the members may choose another chairman and continue the meeting.

The exception to this is in the event of serious disorder, which means something serious enough to prevent the meeting being properly conducted and the views of the members properly ascertained. In this event, the chairman can and should adjourn on his own authority. This is an inherent right which exists regardless of anything to the contrary in the articles. The length of the adjournment should be the minimum period necessary and convenient in the circumstances, perhaps just a few minutes but perhaps to another day.

The chairman may also adjourn on his own authority to facilitate the proceedings. A possible example of this would be to allow a poll to be efficiently conducted.

Directors and auditors

386 Is there anything to stop the members springing a surprise nomination for director on the directors?

Yes, there is. Reg. 76 of Table A states:

'No other person other than a director retiring by rotation shall be appointed or reappointed a director at any general meeting unless:

a) he is recommended by the directors; or

b) not less than fourteen nor more than thirty-five clear days before the date appointed for the meeting, notice executed by a member qualified to vote at the meeting has been given to the company of the intention to propose that person for appointment or reappointment stating the particulars which would, if he were so appointed or reappointed, be required to be included in the company's register of directors together with notice executed by that person of his willingness to be appointed or reappointed.

387 Does retirement by rotation apply in all companies?

Retirement by rotation only applies if and how provision is made for it in the articles. Other arrangements are possible including a situation where directors do not retire at all. In this case, directors continue in office until they die, are removed or become ineligible.

388 How does retirement by rotation operate in detail?

It depends on the articles but Regs. 73 to 75 state the following:

'At the first annual general meeting all the directors shall retire from office, and at every subsequent annual general meeting one-third of the directors who are subject to retirement by rotation or, if their number is not three or a multiple of three, the number nearest to one-third shall retire from office; but, if there is only one director who is subject to retirement by rotation, he shall retire.

Subject to the provisions of the Act, the directors to retire by rotation shall be those who have been longest in office since their last appointment or reappointment, but as between persons who became or were last reappointed directors on the same day those to retire shall (unless they otherwise agree among themselves) be determined by lot.

If the company, at the meeting at which a director retires by rotation, does not fill the vacancy the retiring director shall, if willing to act, be deemed to have been reappointed unless at the meeting it is resolved not to fill the vacancy or unless a resolution for the reappointment of the director is put to the meeting and lost.'

389 I thought that the directors fixed the auditors' remuneration. Am I mistaken?

You are wrong in theory but very probably correct in practice. It is a requirement of the Act that auditors' remuneration be fixed by the members. However, it is very common practice for the resolution to state:

> 'That… be reappointed as auditor for the coming year and that the directors be authorised to fix their remuneration.'

This is very sensible because the directors are more likely to know how much work is involved.

390 What should I know about the appointment or re-appointment of the auditors?

The first auditors may be appointed by the directors but if they do not do so, the first auditors may be appointed by the members in a general meeting. The first auditors hold office until the end of the first meeting at which accounts are laid.

The company is required to appoint an auditor at which accounts are laid. The auditor so appointed will hold office from the end of the meeting until the end of the next meeting at which accounts are laid. There are certain requirements where the auditor to be appointed is not the retiring auditor.

391 What are the special requirements where the auditor to be appointed is not the retiring auditor?

Special formalities apply where a resolution is to be proposed at a general meeting appointing as auditor a person other than a retiring auditor, filling a casual vacancy in the office of auditor, reappointing as auditor a retiring auditor who was appointed by the directors to fill such a vacancy or removing an auditor before the expiration of his term of office.

Special notice of the proposed resolution must be given to the company, and copies of it must then be sent by the company to the auditor proposed to be removed or not re-appointed, and to the auditor that it is proposed to appoint. If the proposed appointment is to fill a casual vacancy, a copy must also be sent to the auditor whose resignation caused the vacancy. An auditor who is to be removed or not re-appointed may have his views circulated to the members and may attend and speak at the meeting. An auditor who has been removed is also entitled to receive notice of and to attend and speak at the general meeting at which his term office would have otherwise expired and any general meeting at which it proposed to fill the vacancy caused by his removal.

Voting

392 In what circumstances is voting conducted by a show of hands?

Unless the articles provide otherwise, which Table A does not, voting in the first instance will normally be by a show of hands. Reg. 46 of Table A provides that a resolution put to the meeting shall be decided on a show of hands, unless a poll is validly decided before the conducting of the vote on a show of hands or on the declaration of the result of a vote on a show of hands.

393 Who can vote on a show of hands?

Subject to the articles, each member personally present and entitled to vote may do so. The duly authorised representative of a corporation may vote. Unless the articles specify otherwise a proxy may not vote on a show of hands, and unless the articles specify otherwise the first named of joint members may vote on all the jointly held shares.

394 How is voting on a show of hands conducted?

It is necessary for the chairman to be clear about who can vote and who cannot. This may be obvious but it may be necessary to do something like issuing coloured cards to those entitled to vote. It is tempting to say that it is one vote per hand but it would be better to say that it is one vote per person. Anyone showing both hands is cheating. Each person only has one vote, regardless of weighted voting or the number of shares that he holds. A member who is a proxy for other members has just one vote. Unless the articles specify otherwise a non-member who is a proxy for members may not vote.

It is the chairman's duty to count the votes and announce the result. He may count the votes himself or he may appoint tellers to help him. If the result is obvious, it may not be necessary to conduct a detailed count. If it is not an ordinary resolution and it is passed on a show of hands, the chairman should say that it has been passed as a different sort of resolution. For example, he should say "I declare that the resolution has been passed as a special resolution".

395 How is a poll demanded?

Section 373 of the Act gives minimum rights about calling a poll. Articles can make it easier but not more difficult. If they purport to do so, the Act takes precedence. Section 373 specifies that:

a)   articles cannot exclude the right to demand a poll (except on the election of the chairman of a meeting or on the adjournment of a meeting); and

b)   articles cannot make a demand ineffective if made by:

i)   at least five members entitled to vote, or

ii)   members holding 10 per cent or more of the voting rights of all the members having the right to vote at the meeting, or

iii) members holding shares on which 10 per cent or more of the total paid up capital has been paid.

Section 373 also specifies that a proxy may join in the demand for a poll. This means that a proxy acting for the necessary number of members can require a poll to be held even if voting on a show of hands was unanimous.

Articles frequently do make it easier to demand a poll. Table A provides that the chairman alone can call for a poll and so can two members entitled to vote.

396 How long is allowed before a poll is taken?

It depends on the articles. Table A gives discretion to the chairman but specifies an upper time limit of 30 days. Table A also specifies that a poll on a motion to adjourn or the election of the chairman must be taken at once. It also specifies that other business may be conducted before the poll is taken.

397 How is voting on a poll conducted?

It depends on the articles. Reg. 49 of Table A gives discretion to the chairman, which he must of course use in the interests of the company and its members. Reg. 49 states:

> 'A poll shall be taken as the chairman directs and he may appoint scrutineers (who need not be members) and fix a time and place for declaring the result of the poll. The result of the poll shall be deemed to be the resolution of the meeting at which the poll was demanded.'

It is usual to make everyone casting a vote in a poll sign a voting slip. This is to forestall mistakes or fraud. A member may vote on a poll even if he was not present at the preceding vote on a show of hands and the calling of a poll. Subject to due process a member may appoint a proxy to vote in a poll even though no proxy was appointed for the preceding vote and the calling of a poll. Several resolutions may be entered on a single voting paper but voting on them must be done individually. It is not permitted to require a voter to approve or reject all the resolutions with a single vote.

In a poll each member may cast all the votes that he has. In a company with a share capital this usually means one vote per share, though some form of weighted voting may be encountered. So normally a member holding 51 per cent of the shares can secure the passage of an ordinary resolution, and a member holding 75 per cent of the shares can secure the passage of an extraordinary or special resolution.

BOARD MEETINGS

General

398 Are matters at a board meeting settled by a majority vote?

Directors may be willing to follow the wishes of a dominant director, but in so doing they are in effect informally voting in a certain way and the majority decides.

When matters are settled formally there is the normal presumption that it is one director one vote, and that victory goes to the side that has the majority. This is certainly the effect of Reg. 88 of Table A. It occasionally happens that company articles specify different arrangements. For example, articles may specify that some things can only happen if the directors are unanimous or there is 75 per cent in favour. Just possibly, articles may provide that the directors are appointed by different groups and that for some items of business a majority is required within each group. Nevertheless, in the great majority of cases it is correct to say that matters are decided by a majority vote.

399 Who is the chairman of the board of directors?

There is no requirement that a board has a chairman and some do not, but most do. Articles may vary, but Reg. 91 of Table A permits the directors to choose a chairman and at any time to remove him from the position. The office of chairman may be held until the appointment is terminated by resignation or by the directors, or it may be for just one meeting. Minutes should make clear the duration of the appointment. Reg. 91 also provides that if the chairman is not willing to act or is not present after five minutes from the appointed time of the meeting, the directors present may appoint one of their number to be chairman of the meeting.

400 Does the chairman have a casting vote at a board meeting?

This is not automatically the case and the chairman only has a casting vote if it is provided by the articles. Reg. 88 of Table A does give the chairman a second or casting vote in the event of a tie and this is the position in most companies. The chairman's casting vote is more likely to be used in a board meeting than in a general meeting. This is because there are usually less votes cast and it is usually one person one vote. The chairman does therefore have quite a lot of power.

401 What are the chairman's powers and duties at a board meeting?

Unless the articles specify differently, the chairman has a casting vote in addition to his normal vote. The chairman only has a casting vote if one is provided by the articles, and Table A does so provide. If the articles do not provide a casting vote, a resolution that results in a tied vote will fail. Table A provides that the chairman's ruling on the right of any director to vote, except himself, shall be final and conclusive.

It is the chairman's duty to manage the proceedings of the board. Much of this is common sense and his actions are subject to the consent of the majority of the directors, but it will include:

- Taking the lead in calling meetings, fixing the agenda and circulating papers ahead of the meeting.

- Generally running the meeting.

- Keeping order and permitting all directors to exercise their rights, including the right to speak.

- Determining who can speak at any one time.

- Calling and managing votes and declaring the results.

- Arranging for minutes to be taken and signed.

The chairman's duty to fairly manage the meeting does not prevent him exercising his own rights. He may speak and vote as he sees fit.

402 Who or what determines the rules for the conduct of board meetings?

Reg. 88 of Table A provides that:

> *'Subject to the provisions of the articles, the directors may regulate their proceedings as they see fit.'*

This gives a great deal of power to the directors themselves and it is (or should be) the wishes of the majority of the directors that prevail. The articles may give instructions and if they do, they should be followed. The general right of directors to set their own rules is of course subject to the dictates of statutory law, though there are not too many requirements. One of them is the obligation to take and keep minutes. It is not open to the directors to decide to rely on the chairman's memory.

As you would expect there are many common law cases interpreting these requirements. For example, in *Clark v Workman 1920* it was held that the appointment of a chairman not made according to the provisions of the articles was void, and that accordingly a decision reached due to the chairman's casting vote was inoperative. In *Browne v La Trinidad 1887* it was held that notice of a board meeting need not be given in writing unless it was a requirement of the articles.

403 What number is a quorum for a board meeting?

It depends on the articles. Reg. 89 of Table A provides that the directors themselves may fix the number of a quorum but if they do not do so, it is two. Reg. 89 also provides that a person who holds office only as an alternate director shall, if his appointer is not present, be counted in the quorum. One person can constitute a quorum if this is permitted by the articles. Directors can only be counted in a quorum if they are able to vote. This means, for example, that unless the articles provide differently, a director who has declared a material personal interest cannot be counted in a quorum.

404 What happens when the number of directors falls below the number needed for a quorum?

This can happen due to death, resignations, etc and what can be done depends on the articles. Reg. 90 of Table A provides that the continuing directors or director may act only for the purposes of filling vacancies or calling a general meeting. If there are no directors left, the members may call a meeting that will appoint new directors.

It can happen that a quorum is present at the start of a meeting but the number drops during the meeting to a number less than is needed for a quorum. Normally this means that business conducted whilst a quorum is present is valid but that any business conducted whilst a quorum is not present is not valid. However, articles can vary this and it is possible for the articles to provide that all business is valid so long as a quorum was present at the start of the meeting.

405 Can a board operate entirely by means of written resolutions?

Yes, it can, though there is something to be said for an actual meeting from time to time. Written resolutions of directors are valid so long as they are signed by every director. They become effective as soon as the last signature is obtained.

406 What matters can a board delegate to a committee?

Unless the articles say differently very many things can be delegated to committees, including a committee of one. Reg. 72 of Table A reads as follows:

> 'The directors may delegate any of their powers to any committee consisting of one or more directors. They may also delegate to any managing director or any director holding any other executive office such of their powers as they consider desirable to be exercised by him. Any such delegation may be made subject to any conditions the directors may impose, and either collaterally with or to the exclusion of their own powers and may be revoked or altered. Subject to any such conditions, the proceedings of a committee with two or more members shall be governed by the articles regulating the proceedings of directors so far as they are capable of applying.'

It is good practice for the setting up of committees, their composition and powers, that the arrangements should be formally minuted. Some matters should be reserved for the full board. The Combined Code envisages audit, remuneration and nomination committees, and states that the appointment and removal of the company secretary should be a matter for the board as a whole.

407 Can any director call a board meeting?

Yes, subject to the articles any director can call a board meeting and the company secretary must do so if instructed by any director.

408 What period of notice is required for a board meeting and in what form must the notice be given?

It is possible that articles may give instructions on these matters, but in the absence of this reasonable notice must be given. What is reasonable notice depends on individual circumstances. If all the directors are readily available, it is probable that a short period of notice is all that is required. If the directors are widely scattered and very busy, a longer period would probably be reasonable. Unless the articles say differently, there is no requirement that notice be given in writing, or indeed in any other particular manner.

409 May a person who is not a director be allowed to attend a board meeting?

Subject to the articles, yes – and it does often happen, either for a whole meeting or just part of it. Employees not on the board and consultants are just two examples of people who might attend. Such people are there by invitation of the board and the invitation may be revoked. Minutes should state the names of people who were present and state that they were there in an advisory capacity, and indeed give details of the advice that they gave. In no circumstances whatsoever should they vote or count towards a quorum.

There is a risk that attendance at board meetings could be a factor leading to a person being a shadow director, but if the above advice is followed it should not happen. Professionals, such as insolvency specialists usually know the risks and insist on acting in the way described.

410 Can a valid board meeting be held using the telephone?

Yes, it can and it is quite common. Reg. 88 of Table A states that the directors may regulate their proceedings as they see fit and it is probable that this is sufficient authority. However, there are no statutory provisions so it depends on the articles and common law. It is just possible that there could be a problem if there is a quorum requirement higher than the number in one place, though this has not been tested. To put it beyond all doubt some companies adopt a special article. Regardless of the articles, only a conference call will do and all directors must be able to hear each other and speak to each other at all times. A series of calls or the chairman relaying messages are not permitted.

411 Can a board meeting be held without all the directors being informed?

The answer is no in most circumstances. However, Reg. 88 of Table A provides that it is not necessary to give notice to a director who is absent from the United Kingdom. Giving notice should of course be interpreted reasonably, such as writing to directors at their notified residential addresses, and the period of notice should be reasonable in the circumstances. It is not open to a director to prevent board meetings being held by taking a long holiday and not leaving a forwarding address.

It is not absolutely clear what is the extent of a director's rights if a meeting is held without him being informed. It is probable that his right is to seek a second meeting. If he does not do this within a reasonable time of discovering that a meeting has been held, the business conducted at the meeting will stand.

412 How frequently should the board meet?

There is no single correct answer to this question. However, all companies, even dormant companies, must have at least one board meeting a year. This is because all companies' accounts must be formally approved by the directors – though this, like any other business, may be done by means of a written resolution. Certain other things also require a formal board decision, though they may not be done in a particular year or indeed at all. Apart from this it is a matter for the directors. Some boards meet relatively infrequently and reserve board meetings for formal business, with the day to day running of the company left to the managers or to the directors working outside the structure of formal board meetings. In other companies the directors meet frequently and actively run the company through these regular meetings.

413 What further part in a board meeting can a director play once he has declared a material interest in a matter under discussion?

Once again it depends on the articles. If Table A applies, the director does not have to leave the meeting whilst the matter is discussed but does not count towards a quorum. He can speak in the discussion but not vote. However, as a matter of courtesy and good practice a director may decide to leave the meeting. Articles may and sometimes do vary these requirements, and may allow a director who has declared an interest to vote. However, articles may not relax the requirements for a director to declare an interest. A director does of course have the right to attend and vote during the parts of a meeting that deal with matters other than the one on which he has declared an interest.

414 Can a formal board meeting ratify the business done at an informal meeting?

Yes, it can. This was established in the case *Re Portuguese Consolidated Copper Mines 1889*.

415 I am sure that there have been many interesting cases about board meetings. Would you tell me about one of them?

Certainly – you are almost bound to find *Barron v Potter 1914* interesting. A company had just two directors and they met by chance at a railway station. Following a casual conversation one director, against the wishes of the other, decided that it had been a board meeting and acted on that basis. It was held that it was not a valid board meeting.

416 I have read the questions and answers in this section about board meetings and in many respects my board does not operate in the required way. Does it matter?

You are not the first person to make this observation and you will probably be aware that in practice many of the requirements are disregarded in some companies – perhaps as a deliberate intention and perhaps due to ignorance. Does it matter? – maybe. The first point to make is that you very probably want to comply with the law, your articles and good practice. You would expect this book to advise you to get it right and that is indeed the advice offered. The second point is that in some cases the rules may actually be being followed. A conscious decision to accept irregularities may perhaps legitimise them. On no account should this argument be stretched too far. You (and others) should know the requirements so that any decision to disregard them is a conscious one and not an unconscious one.

When a requirement is disregarded it is sometimes said 'who knows and who cares?', to which the answer may be 'very few and no-one'. Often no harm is done so long as no-one complains, but do not depend on this too readily as complaints may be raised later. It is not unknown for vengeful former spouses to seek revenge, and directors may be friends at the time but fall out later. If the company is or becomes insolvent, it may matter a great deal. It may cause problems with due diligence if the company is later sold. Of course some irregularities are more serious than others and some are unacceptable in any circumstances.

Irregularities are least likely to be acceptable in listed companies, and they are very undesirable in certain types of company, charities being an example. They are perhaps most likely to be tolerated in a small private company where the directors trust each other and are the major shareholders. Even in a company such as this the rights of minorities should be respected.

Good board meetings

417 Can you suggest a good system for the scheduling of a board meeting and preparation for it?

It is a matter of opinion but there are considerable advantages in scheduling the dates a long time in advance, perhaps a year or more in advance. This helps the directors, especially non-executive directors, book holidays, schedule other meetings, etc. The dates could be individually selected or they could be something like '10.00 am on the first Tuesday in each month'. Listed companies invariably schedule board meetings in this way. The board should normally keep to the scheduled dates, but they can be changed later. If necessary an emergency meeting can be arranged at short notice.

Good meetings often depend on good preparation so the agenda and supporting papers, such as reports, management accounts, etc, should be circulated in good time. It may be necessary for the chairman to be firm about this because some directors may not co-operate, although they are likely to agree in theory. Of course exceptions can be made for emergencies, but not too many of them should be allowed.

418 Have you any other suggestions that may help facilitate good board meetings?

Once again it is a matter of opinion and many disagree, but some degree of formality is desirable. Directors should respect the authority of the chairman and occasionally, if necessary, be required to do so. Of course, the chairman should have the personal qualities that deserve respect. Meetings should be held around a boardroom table rather than with the directors sitting on sofas or something similar.

The directors should try hard to remove themselves from interruptions and meeting away from company premises can help. Staff should know that interruptions will only be tolerated in very exceptional circumstances. The death penalty should be mandatory for not switching off a mobile phone. If there are thirteen directors and one takes a ten minute phone break, a collective two hours are wasted and the quality of the meeting is diminished.

419 We hardly ever have a formal vote at our board meetings. Have we got it wrong?

First of all let's be absolutely clear, the majority decides. Any director is entitled to insist on votes being taken, even if they result in him being in a perpetual minority of one. That said, practices vary according to the wishes of the directors and the dynamics of the board. It can make a big difference if there is a dominant person on the board, perhaps because he owns many or all of the shares.

Sometimes a vote is not taken because the directors are obviously all of the same mind. In this case the chairman just states the decision which is minuted. Sometimes a vote is not taken because, although there is not unanimity, it is clear what the majority want and a formal count is not necessary. Once again the chairman states the decision which is minuted. You may be familiar with a board where a dominant personality states what he has decided, either with or without listening to points of view. The other directors then acquiesce in his decision. By doing this they are in effect asserting their rights to be 'yes men'. Finally, there are boards where the chairman guides the board to a genuine consensus that may or may not end in a formal vote.

There are things to be said for and against all of the dynamics described, though dictatorship tends to be more attractive if you are the dictator. President Abraham Lincoln once submitted a proposal to his cabinet and found that everyone was against him. He called a vote and announced the result as "The ayes one, the noes eleven, the ayes are in the majority".

MINUTES

General

420 Must minutes of meetings be taken and kept?

Yes, they must. Section 382 of the act states:

> 'Every company shall cause minutes of all proceedings of general meet-
> ings, all proceedings at meetings of its directors and, where there are
> managers, all proceedings at meetings of its managers to be entered
> in books kept for that purpose.'

The same section states that if it is not done the company and every officer
in default is liable to a fine and, for continued contravention to a daily default
fine.

421 Who has responsibility for the minutes?

Unless the articles say differently it is the directors, and they have almost
total discretion about who does it and how it is done. This applies to both
general meetings and board meetings. Of course it is generally accepted
that the minutes are the responsibility of the company secretary, but this
is only the case if it is the wish of the directors. The directors can do it
themselves or depute one of their number to do it. They can also ask a
member of staff to attend a meeting and take the minutes, or they can bring
in an outsider for the purpose.

422 What does Table A say about minutes?

Table A says very little on minutes and some of what it does say dupli-
cates the requirements specified in the Act. Reg. 100 of Table A states:

> 'The directors shall cause minutes to be made in books kept for the
> purpose:
>
> a)   of all appointments of officers made by the directors; and

b) *of all proceedings at meetings of the company, of the holder of any class of shares in the company, and of the directors, and of committees of directors, including the names of the directors present at each such meeting.'*

The only specific requirements are that the minutes must give details of appointments made by the directors and the names of directors present, though in practice some sort of attendance register is acceptable and the names need not be recorded in the actual minutes. Beyond this it is down to common law, good practice and the wishes of those concerned.

423 What should be recorded in the minutes?

This is a difficult question to answer and an impossible question to answer conclusively. This is because it is not specified by the Act and it is a matter of opinion. Any specific requirements of the articles should of course be followed. Minutes should record the names of the people present, though it is permissible to record them in some sort of attendance register. They should also record the date of the meeting and the type of meeting (annual general meeting, extraordinary general meeting, directors' meeting, etc). The name of the chairman should be recorded and key events such as adjournments, etc.

It is essential that all resolutions be listed, together with whether or not they were passed. If a resolution was passed as a special resolution or some other particular sort of resolution, this fact should be recorded. It is not necessary to record the number of votes for and against, though it is sometimes done, and of course the number of votes is not always actually counted at a meeting.

How much detail should be included is a matter of opinion. Many people believe that minutes should normally record the key facts and decisions made, and little if anything else. This happens to be the opinion of the writer. On the other hand some people believe that minutes should be much fuller and record what was said as well as what was decided. This type of minutes is harder to take and it may be hard to ensure that it is an impartial record. This is because it is almost inevitable that some views must be summarised, condensed or left out.

There are times when minutes should be fuller than a bald record of the decisions reached. This would be desirable when it is necessary to show why decisions were taken. An example of this might be a directors' meeting in a company facing financial difficulties. The directors might fear an accusation that they carried on trading beyond the point that trading should have stopped, and would want to show that they took proper advice and considered the implications of their decisions.

Minutes should of course be impartial.

424 How can a mistake in the minutes be corrected after they have been signed?

Minutes should not be altered after they have been signed. If an error is subsequently discovered it should be dealt with by means of a subsequent minute.

425 Is it a requirement that minutes be kept in a bound book?

No, this is not a legal requirement although minutes are often kept in this traditional way. It is also permissible and very common for minutes to be kept in a loose-leaf binder. Section 722 of the Act permits minutes to be kept in computerised form, though it is a requirement that the system is capable of printing out written copies. Although permissible this does pose practical problems concerning signature, verification, etc.

426 Is it necessary to enter written resolutions of the members or directors in the minute book, and is it necessary to record informal corporate acts by the members in the minute book?

Written resolutions must be entered in the minute book. Informal corporate acts of members should be entered in the minute book if they are of a nature that require it. This of course may well present practical difficulties.

427 What are the legal requirements when there is a sole director or sole member?

Minutes must still be kept and it is the duty of the sole member or sole director to provide signed minutes. This applies to any formal meeting at which the one person was the sole voting person present, any written resolution of the sole member or sole director, and any decision taken informally by the sole member or sole director that is required to be minuted.

Approval and afterwards

428 What is the correct system for approving the minutes?

This is not specified by the Act and it is not specified by Table A, though individual company articles may direct what must happen. If they do, the requirements should be observed. Minutes must be taken and kept, but unless the articles give directions, a great deal of freedom is allowed concerning the method of approval. It is not even a requirement that the minutes be signed, though in practice this is almost always done, and for good reasons.

In the opinion of the writer, the person taking the minutes should try to produce them shortly after the meeting. It is best to do this whilst the events are still fresh in his mind, and in the minds of the chairman and others that he might consult. Draft minutes should be circulated as soon after the meeting as possible and before the meeting at which they are to be approved. Approval of the minutes of a directors' meeting should be the first item of business at the next directors' meeting. Discussion should hopefully be brief or non-existent. If there is a discussion, the chairman should ensure that it is confined to the accuracy of the record. A re-run of the discussion at the last meeting should not be allowed. If there is an inaccuracy, it should be corrected prior to signature. A quick vote or informal acceptance should be followed by the chairman's signature.

In the opinion of the writer the minutes of a general meeting should be approved in the same way at the board meeting following the general meeting. In some companies it is the practice for the minutes of one annual general meeting to be approved a year later at the following annual general meeting. This practice has little to commend it and a great deal can be said against it. Many people will have forgotten what happened and some or all of the members present may not have been members at the time of the meeting in question.

429 Are duly signed minutes conclusive evidence of what happened at a meeting?

No, the evidence is very strong but not conclusive. Section 382 of the Act specifies that minutes signed by the chairman of the meeting at which the business was transacted, or by the chairman of the next succeeding meeting, are evidence of the proceedings and that the meeting has been duly convened and held, unless the contrary is proved. Signed minutes are prima-facie evidence but may be set aside by the court. This could be done, for example, if fraud is proved or an obvious error is shown. This could be, for example, the total number of votes cast being recorded as greater than the total number of votes available to be cast.

430 Is it necessary to keep the minutes of directors' meetings separate from the minutes of members' meetings?

It is a good idea because members may inspect the minutes of members' meetings, but may only inspect the minutes of directors' meetings with the consent of the directors.

ten

Accounts and audit 431-460

ten

Accounts and audit

Accounts

431 Whose responsibility is it to prepare, lay and deliver the accounts?

It is the directors' responsibility.

432 What are the procedures for approving, signing, laying and delivering the accounts?

Directors are required to keep proper accounting records and to prepare, or have prepared, statutory accounts. It is specifically required that the accounts be approved by the board, either by a majority vote at a board meeting or by means of a unanimous written resolution. In approving the accounts the directors are of course signifying their belief that the accounts are accurate and comply with the law, not that they are pleased with the figures.

After approval any director signs the balance sheet, and any director or the company secretary signs the directors' report and the directors' remuneration report, if there is one. The audit report, if there is one, is then signed by the auditor. It is normal for three sets of the accounts to be signed in ink, one for Companies House, one for the auditor to keep and one for the directors to keep. Further sets as required are produced with printed names rather than signatures.

The accounts must be sent to the members and any others entitled to receive them. Unless an appropriate elective resolution is in force they must be laid before the members in a general meeting. It is usual for this to be done at the annual general meeting, but it can be done at an extraordinary general meeting. A copy of the accounts must be sent to the Registrar of Companies, who will put them on the public record at Companies House. Subject to certain conditions, unlimited companies are not required to deliver accounts to the Registrar.

433 What is the composition of a set of accounts?

A set of accounts comprise the following:

- A profit and loss account or, in the case of a company not trading for profit, an income and expenditure account.

- A balance sheet made up as at the last date of the profit and loss (or income and expenditure) period.

- A directors' report.

- An auditors' report (if required).

- A consolidated profit and loss account and consolidated balance sheet (if required).

- A directors' remuneration report (in the case of quoted companies only).

If a consolidated profit and loss account is required, a profit and loss account for the company alone is not obligatory.

434 What are the requirements for a dormant company?

The directors of dormant companies must sign, lay and deliver accounts in the same way as required for active companies. Such accounts may, subject to circumstances, be extremely simple and can just consist of a balance sheet containing two figures (share capital and cash). Companies House provides a voluntary form which may be used for this purpose.

A dormant company may dispense with an audit if all the following conditions apply:

- It must qualify as a 'small company' for the accounts period in which it became dormant.

- It has been dormant since the end of that accounts period.

- It was not required to prepare group accounts for the period.

- It is not a banking or insurance company, and it is not authorised under the Financial Services Act.

- It has not made any significant accounting transactions at all in the period.

435 What are the special rules for the period of a company's first accounts?

A company's first accounts must cover a period not less than six months and not more than 18 months. If the period of the first accounts is more than 12 months, the period allowed for laying and delivering is 10 months (seven months for plcs) from the first anniversary of incorporation of the company, or three months from the end of the first accounting reference period, whichever is the later.

436 Is it compulsory that accounts comply with accounting standards?

No, it is not compulsory, though nearly all accounts do comply. Accounts must comply with all applicable accounting standards unless, exceptionally, the directors decide not to do so. If the directors do make this decision, they must disclose which accounting standards have not been followed and their reasons for not doing so. If the accounts are audited, the auditor will express an opinion about the effect and significance of the departure from the accounting standards. The directors' reasons may be good, bad or a matter of opinion. Everything, including compliance with accounting standards, is subsidiary to the requirement that the accounts should give a true and fair view.

Decisions not to comply with accounting standards are relatively rare. This is partly because accounting standards are well-respected, but also because it leads to qualified audit reports and possibly to searching questions from the Inland Revenue, the bank, members and others.

437 What are the definitions of small and medium-sized companies?

The following definitions apply for accounting periods ending on or after 30th January 2004. Small and medium-sized companies must satisfy any two out of the following three conditions (counted on a group basis).

	Turnover	Balance sheet total	Average number of employees
Small	£5.6 million net (or £6.72 million gross)	£2.8 million net (or £3.36 million gross)	50
Medium-sized	£22.8 million net (or £27.36 million gross)	£11.4 million net (or £13.68 million gross)	250

Public companies do not qualify for exemptions and neither do banking companies, insurance companies and an 'authorised person' under the Financial Services Act 1986.

438 What are the benefits of being a small or medium-sized company?

Small and medium-sized companies may file abbreviated accounts at Companies House though there is no compulsion for them to do so. They must still provide full accounts to their members, so there is no saving in work preparing the accounts and in fact the opposite is the case. The benefit is privacy because, if it is so wished, less information is put into the public domain. At the time of writing small and medium-sized companies enjoy certain tax advantages relating to capital allowances.

439 What exemptions are available for abbreviated accounts?

The exemptions for a small company are:

- No profit and loss account need be filed.

- No directors' report need be filed.

- The balance sheet and notes to the accounts may be summarised.

The exemptions for a medium-sized company only cover the profit and loss account, not the balance sheet. The profit and loss account need not disclose the turnover, cost of sales and other operating income.

440 What is the accounting reference date and what is its significance?

Every company has an accounting reference date. The initial accounting reference date is allocated by Companies House and it is the last day of the month in which the company is registered. So, for example, companies registered on 4th April and 18th April will both be given the accounting reference date of 30th April. The period between two accounting reference dates is the accounting reference period. The significance of the accounting reference date is that accounts must be made up to a date within seven days either side of it. So, for example, if the accounting reference date is 30th April, the balance sheet may be dated any day between 23rd April and 7th May.

441 Can the accounting reference date be changed?

Yes, it can. It is a decision of the directors and they must notify Companies House by means of form 225. The consequence of doing so is that the accounts do not cover a period of a year.

The directors may freely bring the accounting reference date forward so that the accounts period is less than a year. They can do this as often as they wish. They can put back the accounting reference date so that the accounts period is longer than a year, but there are two conditions that must always be met:

- The accounts period can never be longer than 18 months.

- The accounts must not be overdue unless the company is subject to an administration order.

Furthermore, the accounting reference date cannot be put back more than once in a five year period unless one of the following exceptions applies:

- The company is subject to an administration order.

- The approval of the Secretary of State has been obtained.

- The change is to align the date with that of a parent or subsidiary established in the European Economic Area.

- The company is an oversea company.

442 Is there a way round the restrictions on changing the accounting reference date?

Yes, there is and it is a glaring anomaly. However, it cannot be done if the resulting accounts period is longer than 18 months or if the accounts are overdue. Subject to this it can be done in four steps as follows:

1. Buy an off-the-shelf, dormant subsidiary company.

2. Change the accounting reference date of the subsidiary company to the required date.

3. Change your accounting reference date to match that of the dormant subsidiary.

4. Have the dormant subsidiary company struck-off.

This achieves the desired result at a cost of less than £100.

443 What are the time limits for laying and delivering the accounts?

The time limits are the same for laying the accounts before the members and delivering them to the Registrar of Companies. Counting from the accounting reference date, it is seven months for a PLC and ten months for a private company. It is six months for listed companies but this is a requirement of the listing rules, not a Companies Act requirement. The dates for delivering accounts to the Registrar are strictly interpreted. For example, 10 months from 28th February is 28th December, not 31st December.

444 Is it possible for the time limits to be extended?

It is possible if the accounting period commenced on or before 31st December 2004 and if the company carries on business or has interests outside the United Kingdom, the Channel Islands and the Isle of Man. Having exports, no matter how small the amount, is sufficient to qualify. The directors may claim a three months extension, making it 10 months for a PLC and 13 months for a private company. They do this by submitting form 244 to the Registrar of Companies. The form must be submitted before the accounts are overdue and it only applies for just one year.

The possible three months extention has now been withdrawn and it is not available for accounting periods commencing on or after 1st January 2005.

445 What are the penalties for laying and delivering the accounts late?

It is an offence for the directors, and one or more of them may be prosecuted and fined. However, prosecutions are relatively rare and usually only happen when the offence is particularly bad. A director may put forward the defence that he took all reasonable steps to secure compliance and it will be up to the court whether or not this is accepted.

Separately, Companies House will almost invariably impose civil penalties if accounts are delivered late. These are a civil matter, not a criminal conviction, and are levied on the company, not the directors. The scale of the penalties is:

Length of period	Public company	Private company
Not more than 3 months	£500	£100
Between 3 and 6 months	£1,000	£250
Between 6 and 12 months	£2,000	£500
More than 12 months	£5,000	£1,000

Audit

446 What is the requirement to have accounts audited?

The accounts of all PLCs must be audited and so must the accounts of all private companies that are part of a group that has contained a PLC at any time during the year.

For accounts periods ending on or after 30th March 2004 an audit is not compulsory for other private companies, provided that they meet **all** the following criteria:

- It must be a 'small company'. The definition of a small company is given in the answer to question 437.

- Its balance sheet total must not be greater than £2.8 million.

- Annual turnover must be not more than £5.6 million.

All the figures are counted on a group basis, so a small company that is part of a large group must be audited.

Accounts must be audited if at any time during the year it came under any of the regulatory regimes specified in section 249B of the Act. Such companies include banking or insurance companies, registered insurance brokers, Financial Services Act authorised persons or appointed representatives, trade unions and employers' associations. This covers the great majority of cases but there are more fine-tuning details.

The requirements are different for charitable companies and dormant companies, and details for charitable companies are given in the answer to the next question.

447 Is the requirement different for companies that are charitable companies?

Most of the requirements are the same as described in the answer to the previous question. However, the turnover limit is £90,000 rather than £5.6 million. Charitable companies having a turnover between £90,000 and £250,000 may submit an accountant's compilation report as an alternative to an audit. Charitable companies having a turnover greater than £250,000 are required to have their accounts audited. Also the balance sheet total for a charitable company is £1.4 million rather than £2.8 million.

The Government has published a draft Charities Bill. If and when it is enacted as published, there will be no change to the £90,000 turnover limit, but the upper limits for a compilation report will be raised to £500,000 for turnover and £2.8 million for the balance sheet total.

448 Can the members insist on having an audit?

Yes, they can. Members holding a minimum of 10 per cent in nominal value of a company's issued share capital, or any class of it, may require its accounts to be audited. This would include the holders of 10 per cent of a class of non-voting preference shares. If a company does not have a share capital, it is 10 per cent of its members.

449 What are the main duties of an auditor?

An auditor's main duty is to report on the company's statutory accounts, and in particular to give an opinion (not a certificate) as to whether the balance sheet gives a 'true and fair view'. Closely allied to this is a duty to report on any non-disclosure in the accounts of information regarding directors' emoluments, employees' emoluments, substantial contracts with directors and loans to directors. They must also consider whether or not the information given in the directors' report is consistent with the corresponding accounts.

450 Does the auditor have any other duties?

Yes, there are other duties, though you may well not encounter them. They include:

- Making and/or reporting on expert valuations of assets where shares are paid up by non-cash consideration; the report could also be given by any person qualified to be the auditor of the company.

- Auditing interim accounts preliminary to the payment of certain dividends.

- Making statements in connection with the re-registration of a private company as a public company.

- Reporting in connection with the giving by a private company of financial assistance for the acquisition of its own shares.

- Reporting in connection with the purchase by a private company of its own shares out of capital.

- Giving a statement of opinion in a summary financial statement issued by a public listed company concerning consistency of the summary statement with the report and accounts and auditors' report.

451 Who and what can audit companies?

An auditor must be accorded the status of a registered auditor by one of the Registered Supervisory Bodies. It is not sufficient to just be a member of a Registered Supervisory Body. The Registered Supervisory Bodies are the Chartered Accountants Institutes of England and Wales, Scotland and Ireland, the Association of Chartered Certified Accountants and the Association of Authorised Public Accountants. A partnership or body corporate may be appointed auditor provided that it is qualified to be so appointed. Officers and employees of a company cannot be its auditor, and neither can their partners or any partnership in which any such person is a partner. Partner in this sense means a business partner rather than a live-in companion.

452 Who appoints the auditor and fixes their remuneration, and how is it done?

The first auditor may be appointed by the directors, who may also fix his remuneration. The directors may also make an appointment to fill a casual vacancy and fix the remuneration of the auditor so appointed. An auditor appointed by the directors serves until the conclusion of the next general meeting at which accounts are laid. If the directors fail to appoint a first auditor or fill a casual vacancy, the members in a general meeting may do so.

At each general meeting at which accounts are laid, the members are required to appoint or re-appoint the auditor and fix their remuneration. In practice the members usually pass a resolution that authorises the directors to fix the auditors' remuneration. There are special formalities if it is proposed that an auditor other than the retiring auditor be appointed. An auditor appointed by a meeting of members serves to the end of the next general meeting at which accounts are laid.

If the company fails to make any appointment, the Secretary of State may fill the vacancy and the company is required to inform the Secretary of State within one week after the meeting that her power of appointment has become exercisable.

453 Can the directors remove an auditor?

No, they cannot. This is the prerogative of the members. The directors can submit a resolution to a meeting of the members that provides that an auditor be removed or changed. Special formalities apply if this is done.

454 What rights does an auditor have in connection with members' meetings?

An auditor must be sent all official company notices and related documents, and this includes notice of a members' meeting. An auditor has the right to attend such meetings and speak on any part of the business that concerns them as auditors.

455 How can an auditor be removed?

This question presupposes that the auditor is not willing to resign. In practice auditors are usually willing to resign if they realise that this is probably the wish of many members. If it is wished that the auditor be removed, it can be done by means of an ordinary resolution of the members. The registrar must be informed on form 391 within 14 days. An actual meeting must be held and removal of an auditor cannot be accomplished by means of a written resolution. Special formalities must be followed and these are detailed in the answer to the next question.

456 What are the special formalities that must be followed when an auditor is removed?

They may be summarised as follows:

- Special notice of the proposed resolution must be given to the company.

- On receipt of the special notice, copies must be sent by the company forthwith to the person(s) intended to be appointed, removed or not reappointed as the case may be. Where the filling of a casual vacancy is or was involved, a copy must also be sent to the person whose resignation caused the vacancy.

- The auditor to be removed or not reappointed may make written representations to the company. The company must circulate them with the notice of the meeting. If the representations are received too late for circulation, the auditor may require them to be read out at the meeting. The Court can relieve the company of these obligations if it is satisfied that they contain needlessly defamatory matter.

- The auditor is entitled to attend and speak at the meeting.

- An auditor who has been removed is also entitled to receive notice of and to attend and speak at the general meeting at which his term of office would have otherwise expired, and any general meeting at which it is proposed to fill the vacancy caused by his removal.

457 Must a resigning auditor give reasons for the resignation?

The short answer is no, but the written notice of resignation must be accompanied by a statement that there are no circumstances that should be brought to the attention of the members or creditors of the company, or alternatively by such a statement. If a statement is submitted by the resigning auditor, the company must send a copy to the Registrar of Companies and every person entitled to receive a copy of the statutory accounts. The company may apply to the court for an order restraining publication of a statement received.

A resigning auditor may deposit with his resignation a requisition ordering the directors to convene an extraordinary general meeting of the company to consider his explanation of the circumstances of the resignation.

458 What rights do auditors have to see documents and have their questions answered?

The auditors of a company have a right of access at all times to the company's books, accounts and vouchers, and are entitled to require from the company's officers such information and explanations as they think necessary for the performance of their duties as auditors.

459 Who is required to co-operate with an auditor?

At the time of writing it is the officers of the company, and the officers and auditors of any subsidiary companies. However, the position is likely to be different by the time that these words are read. The Companies (Audit, Investigations and Community Enterprise) Bill (if and when it is enacted and takes effect) will extend the list to the following:

- Any officer of the company. This means all directors, all company secretaries and anyone falling within the definition of 'manager'.

- All employees. Note it is not just senior employees.

- Any person holding or accountable for any of the company's books, accounts or vouchers. This could include, for example, a self-employed accountant or bookkeeper.

- Any subsidiary company that is incorporated in Great Britain. This is the legal entity rather than its officers or employees.

- Any officer, employee, auditor or person holding or accountable for any books, accounts or vouchers of a subsidiary company incorporated in Great Britain.

- Any person who fell into any of the above categories at a time to which the information or enquiries relate. This makes it retrospective and it can, for example, include former employees.

If information is required from a subsidiary company not incorporated in Great Britain, the parent company will be required to take all reasonable steps to try and obtain the information. It is not considered practical to directly try to force subsidiary companies not incorporated in Great Britain to co-operate with British auditors.

460 What are the obligations of the directors to draw relevant matters to the attention of auditors?

Directors have many obligations including obligations to prepare, approve and sign accounts that give a 'true and fair' view, and to submit them to audit unless an exemption applies. They are required to answer auditors' questions and to produce documents required by auditors. However, there is no specific obligation to draw matters to the attention of auditors.

The above is the position at the time of writing but it is likely to be different when these words are read. The Companies (Audit, Investigations and Community Enterprise) Bill is in Parliament, and this requires the directors to include a statement in the directors' report that the directors are not aware of any relevant information which has not been disclosed to the company's auditors.

eleven

Financial difficulties, winding-up and striking off 461-501

eleven

Financial difficulties, winding-up and striking off

FINANCIAL DIFFICULTIES

The position of the directors

461 What should the directors do when they believe that their company may have financial difficulties?

Directors are required to keep proper records and accounts. This is always important but it is especially important if financial difficulties are experienced. Good records and accounts should give early warning of impending trouble and they should give the facts on which a plan of action can be based. The courts recognise that the directors of small private companies may not have the same expertise as the directors of large companies and they may be more tolerant in the case of their failings. Nevertheless, there are minimum standards expected of all directors. All directors should keep proper accounts or pay someone to do it, and they should review the figures.

If problems are indicated, they should do the necessary investigations and projections. If they do not do it themselves, they should commission someone with the necessary expertise. An extremely important point is that they should usually take independent professional advice and they should do so quickly. This should be from a person able to give such advice, very probably a suitably qualified accountant or solicitor. It is possible that the advice will be taken from a Licensed Insolvency Practitioner or that they will be advised to speak to a Licensed Insolvency Practitioner.

462 What should directors not do when they believe that their company may have financial difficulties?

There is obviously quite a list, but two things in particular should be mentioned:

1. They should not carry on trading beyond the point at which trading should stop.

2. They should not exercise undue preference and in particular they should not make payments that unduly prefer their own interests. An example would be to pay off a bank overdraft against which directors' personal guarantees have been given.

There can be great pressure on directors when a company faces financial difficulties. It sometimes happens that directors put all their energies into 'fire fighting' and such things as boosting sales and fending off creditors. This may work but they should not neglect the accounts and their responsibilities.

463 What action might directors take after receiving suitable professional advice?

The following are among the steps that the directors might consider:

*   They could decide (after taking advice) to carry on trading. It may be necessary to explain the problems and the plan to the bank and/or creditors.

*   They could decide to put the company into administration.

*   They could decide to ask the bank to appoint a receiver.

*   They could decide to seek an injection of capital.

*   They could decide to seek an amalgamation or reconstruction.

- They could decide to recommend to the members that the company be voluntarily wound up.

- They could accept that the company must be compulsorily wound up.

464 What personal risks might directors run when a company faces financial difficulties?

One or more of the directors may face personal risks in one or more of five areas:

Personal liability for wrongful trading

This can happen when a company is liquidated and there is not enough money to pay all creditors in full. A court may order one or more directors to make a contribution to the deficiency. This may be done if a director knew or ought to have known that an insolvent liquidation was likely, but failed to stop trading or failed to take reasonable steps to minimise the deficiency.

Disqualification

A director may be disqualified by a court from holding the position of director in any company.

Criminal liability

This can happen if a director breaks one of several laws and in particular is guilty of fraudulent trading. Fraudulent trading can take place even if a company does not go into liquidation.

Personal liability for fraudulent trading

A director guilty of fraudulent trading may be ordered to contribute in the case of winding up. This can only happen if the company is wound up.

Misfeasance

This does not necessarily involve dishonesty, although it may do so. It does involve the wrongful direction or detention of company assets. It may include, for example, paying a dividend out of capital and it may include a director purchasing company assets at a price below their true value.

Administration

465 Why was the concept of administration introduced in 1986?

There existed for many years a general feeling that too many companies were lost that might have been rescued. A company that got into difficulties all too often went into liquidation. This happened either straight away or following receivership. A receiver's primary function was to safeguard the interests of the secured creditors that appointed him. The interests of the company and other creditors were secondary.

This was one of the problems addressed by the Insolvency Act 1986. The Act introduced the concept of administration. One of its features was an interval during which a company had protection from its creditors. This interval was to be used either to turn round the business and save all of it or part of it, or to lead to a winding up on more advantageous terms. There are of course dangers in this and safeguards are necessary, one being that the administrator must be a Licensed Insolvency Practitioner.

466 Yes – but just what is administration?

Administration gives a breathing space to a company in financial difficulties. During this period it is under the control of an administrator (who must be a Licensed Insolvency Practitioner) and not the directors. At the end of the period of administration the company is returned to the control of the directors, or to a liquidator if the company is wound up.

An administration order may be granted by a court or there are out of court routes into administration. Administration is only for one of the purposes described in the answer to question 468. Whilst it is in force creditors may not bring or continue a legal action to recover money due to them, and there are other restrictions too. On no account should an administrator be confused with an administrative receiver. Despite the similarity in names they are completely different.

467 What is a Licensed Insolvency Practitioner?

The Insolvency Act 1986 stipulates that all liquidators, administrators and administrative receivers must be Licensed Insolvency Practitioners. A Licensed Insolvency Practitioner is licensed by the Department of Trade and Industry and holds one of a number of specified professional qualifications. The practitioner is bound to observe professional standards. Complaints are sometimes made about the costs, and occasionally unsatisfactory work is reported. However, professional standards are now maintained. Of course, given that people sometimes lose money in administrations and receiverships, and always lose money in insolvent liquidations, some hard feelings are almost inevitable.

468 What are the permitted purposes of administration?

The administrator must pursue one of three aims:

1. Rescue the company as a going concern.

2. Achieve a better result for the company's creditors as a whole than would be likely if the company were to be wound up (without first being in administration).

3. Realise property in order to make a distribution to one or more secured or preferential creditors.

The administrator is required to pursue the first objective so long as he thinks it reasonably practical to do so. Rescuing the company as a going concern means the company and as much of its business as possible. If he thinks that it is not possible, the second objective ranks ahead of the third objective.

469 Who can apply to have a company put into administration?

Most applications are made by the directors using the out of court route. Out of court routes into administration may be instigated by the company itself, its directors or the holder of a qualifying floating charge.

An application to the court may be made by any of the following or any combination of them acting together:

- The company itself.

- The directors – this means on behalf of the majority, not a minority.

- One or more of the creditors.

- The Justices' Chief Executive who has the responsibility of recovering fines imposed on the company.

470 Is it true that a company can only go into administration if it is unable to pay its debts?

A company may go into administration if it is in breach of the terms of a qualifying floating charge. Apart from this it can only happen if it is unable to pay its debts or is unlikely to be able to pay its debts. The answer to the next question explains what this means.

471 What does 'unable to pay its debts' mean?

It has a legal meaning that differs in different parts of the United Kingdom. It does matter because in most cases a company can only go into administration if it is shown that it is unable to pay its debts, or is unlikely to be able to pay its debts. In England and Wales it means that one of the following applies:

- It has received a demand in the prescribed form for a debt of at least £750, and has not made payment for a period of at least three weeks.

- Execution or other process issued on a judgement decree or order of any court in favour of a creditor of the company is unsatisfied in whole or in part.

- The company is unable to pay its debts as they fall due.

- The amount of the company's assets is less than the amount of its liabilities.

472 What powers does an administrator have?

An administrator has very wide powers that include the following:

- He may appoint and remove directors.
- He takes over the powers formerly exercised by the directors.
- He may call a meeting of members.
- He may borrow money.
- He may use the company seal.
- He may bring actions in the name of the company.
- He may defend actions in the name of the company.
- He may sell company property.

473 What are the consequences of a company going into administration?

The consequences take effect from the time that an application is made. If the application is refused, they cease to apply. The following are the main consequences:

- The company may not be wound up. Any winding up proceedings in progress are frozen.
- No claims for recovery of debts may be commenced and any that are in existence are frozen.
- No steps may be taken to enforce judgments that have been obtained. This includes action by a High Court Sheriff or a county court bailiff.
- Property subject to hire purchase or lease agreements may not be repossessed.
- No security may be enforced. This means, for example, that a bank may not appoint a receiver to safeguard its security.
- No goods subject to retention of title clauses may be repossessed by suppliers.

474 I am a director of a company that is going to go into administration. What will my powers be?

The administrator will run the company and your position will be like that of a manager under his authority. You will have as much power as he allows you to have.

475 I am a director of a company in administration. Can I be dismissed by the administrator?

Yes.

476 One of our customers is in administration. What powers do we have?

Unless the court gives you special permission, which is unlikely, you may not commence legal action to recover money owing to you, legal actions that have commenced are frozen and no goods subject to retention of title clauses may be repossessed. This does not leave you many options but you do not have to make new contracts with your customer and, depending on the strength of your position, this may give you some leverage with the administrator. If you are a key supplier and the administrator needs you badly, you can negotiate from a position of strength. If, on the other hand, you supply mince pies for the Christmas party and it is February, your bargaining power is virtually non-existent. You may just possibly take some comfort from the thought that the administration is for the benefit of the creditors, including you.

477 Is an administrator personally liable for contracts that he makes on behalf of the company?

No, he is not. However, an administrator is a qualified, licensed professional person and it is very unlikely that you would not be paid for orders that he places.

Receivership

478 What is receivership?

An administrative receiver may be appointed under the authority of a fixed charge and, if so, his authority only extends to the assets covered by the fixed charge. On the other hand, an administrative receiver may be appointed under the authority of a floating charge and, if so, his authority extends to all assets and he has the power to run the business. The directors are relieved of their powers for the duration of the receivership.

Most, but not all, administrative receivers are appointed by banks. An administrative receiver must be a Licensed Insolvency Practitioner and his first duty is to the bank (or other lender) that appointed him. His job is to safeguard the secured assets and endeavour to recover the money owing. Receivership often, but not always, leads to the company being wound up.

479 Would you please define an administrative receiver?

Section 29(2) of the Insolvency Act 1986 defines an administrative receiver as:

'a)   *a receiver or manager of the whole (or substantially the whole) of a company's property appointed by or on behalf of the holders of any debentures of the company secured by a charge which, as created, was a floating charge, or by such a charge and one or more other securities; or*

b)   *a person who would be such a receiver or manager but for the appointment of some other person as the receiver of part of the company's property.'*

480 What is the essential difference between administration and receivership?

Administration is for the benefit of all creditors and, if possible, the administrator must rescue the company as a going concern. Receivership is primarily for the benefit of the lender (usually a bank) that appointed the administrative receiver.

481 I have heard that there are more administrations and less receiverships. Why is this?

Administration was introduced by the *Insolvency Act 1986*. It had some successes but it did not achieve all that had been hoped. This was partly because in many cases a receiver was appointed instead of a company going into administration. The holder of a qualifying floating charge, usually a bank, was able to pre-empt administration by appointing a receiver. The balance has been very considerably changed by the *Insolvency Act 2002*. With certain exceptions it is not possible to appoint a receiver under the authority of a floating charge created after 15th September 2003. It is still possible to appoint a receiver under the authority of a qualifying floating charge created prior to 15th September 2003.

The balance has therefore moved decisively towards administration and away from receivership. There will be more administrations and fewer receiverships. However, this will be a trend over several years rather than a sharp change with a cut-off point. This is because a receiver may still be appointed under the authority of a qualifying floating charge created prior to 15th September 2003.

482 How can we stop a receiver being appointed?

The appointment of an administrative receiver is rightly regarded as a defeat for the company and its directors. The following is easy advice to give and may be hard to follow, and it may seem condescending, but:

- The directors should try to keep debenture holders fully informed. The appointment of a receiver is often partly caused by frustration at a lack of information and a feeling that things are being hidden.

- The directors should run the company so that covenants and conditions are not breached. They should be wary of over-trading.

WINDING-UP

General

483 What are the three ways in which a company may be wound up?

The three ways are:

- Members' voluntary winding-up.
- Creditors' voluntary winding-up.
- Winding-up by the court.

484 What are the stages in a winding-up?

This question could have a very long answer but the winding-up procedures can be summarised in four stages as follows:

1. A decision is made to wind up the company. This is made either by the members or by the court.

2. A liquidator, who must be a Licensed Insolvency Practitioner, is appointed. This is done either by the members or the creditors, or if there is no appointment it is the official receiver.

3. The liquidator realises the assets.

4. The liquidator pays out the money to creditors in the order of precedence fixed by law. If creditors are paid in full, any remaining funds are paid to the contributors (members).

485 What is the difference between a members' voluntary winding-up and a creditors' voluntary winding-up?

In both cases the decision to wind up the company is taken by the members. The difference is that in a members' voluntary winding-up the choice of liquidator is made by the members and the proceedings are under their control. In a creditors' voluntary winding up the choice of liquidator is made by the creditors and the proceedings are under their control.

It will be a members' voluntary winding-up if the directors make a declaration of solvency and file it with the Registrar of Companies. This must
state that the directors are of the opinion that the company will be able
to pay all creditors (plus interest at the official rate) within a year of the
commencement of the winding-up. Needless to say, this declaration should
only be made responsibly and after making suitable enquiries.

486 What are acceptable reasons for a members' voluntary winding-up?

The members do not have to have an acceptable reason. The members
own the company and all the creditors will be paid in full, so the members
can have the company wound up when they like for whatever reason they
like.

487 In what circumstances can a company be wound up by the court?

By far the most common reason for a company to be wound up by the
court is that the court has been successfully petitioned by a creditor or
judgment creditor, who is owed at least £750. However, a company may
also be wound-up by the court when any of the following apply:

- The members so request it by means of a special resolution.

- Membership of a public company has fallen below two members.

- A public company has not obtained a trading certificate within
  a year of registration.

- A public company has not commenced trading, or has stopped
  trading for a year.

- It is just and equitable for the company to be wound-up.

- If the company is, was or should have been regulated by the
  Financial Services Authority and winding up is requested by the
  Financial Services Authority.

488 In what circumstances might the court decide that it is just and equitable for a company to be wound up?

The court has a great deal of discretion. Perhaps the most common reason is irreconcilable differences between the members. This can happen, for example, when there are just two members each holding exactly half the shares. They could agree to have the company wound up as a members' winding up, but if this co-operation cannot be achieved, one of them could ask the court to have the company wound up. Another example is where the company has been used for criminal purposes and winding it up is in the public interest.

Order of priority in the distribution of funds

489 My company is insolvent and is being wound up. Who will get what money there is?

Since the abolition of Crown Preference part of the money goes to the ordinary creditors as described in the answer to the next question. Subject to this the order of priority is as follows:

1. The expenses of the liquidation (this includes the liquidator's fees).

2. Preferential debts (but not interest due after the liquidation).

3. Debts secured by a qualifying floating charge (but not interest due after liquidation).

4. Ordinary debts (but not interest due after the liquidation).

5. Interest on preferential and ordinary debts at the statutory rate.

6. The contributors (members).

If the members get anything, the company was not actually insolvent.

490 If a company is insolvent, what part of its money is ring-fenced for ordinary creditors?

The formula for the part of net property to be ring-fenced is as follows:

    i)   50 per cent of the first £10,000

    ii)   20 per cent of the remainder

    iii) But the total amount ring-fenced cannot exceed £600,000

    iv) And nothing may be ring-fenced if the cost of distribution would be disproportionate.

491 Which debts rank as preferential?

Preferential debts (which rank equally between themselves) are:

- Contributions to occupational pension schemes, etc.

- Remuneration, etc of employees – up to a specified limit.

- Levies on coal and steel production.

- Money owing to third parties in connection with debts, which would have been preferential had they not been paid by the third parties.

Debts to the Inland Revenue and HM Customs and Excise no longer rank as preferential.

STRIKING-OFF

Following application by the directors

492 We want to end the registration of a dormant, private company. Is there an alternative to a members' voluntary winding-up?

You could, and probably should, apply to have the company struck-off, which is a quick, cheap and simple alternative to a members' voluntary winding-up. The company must be dormant and solvent. Details of how it is done are given in the answer to question 493 and possible pitfalls are detailed in the answer to question 494. Striking-off is not an option for public companies.

493 What are the steps leading to a voluntary striking-off of a private company?

Application to the Registrar using form 652a must be made by the directors. The form must be accompanied by a payment of £10 which is the only charge. The application may be made by a sole director, both of them if the company has two, or the majority if the company has more than two. Within the previous three months the company must not have traded or otherwise carried on business, or changed its name. Also, it must not be the subject or proposed subject of insolvency proceedings or a compromise or arrangement with members or creditors. The applicant directors must give a copy of form 652a to every member of the company, employee of the company, creditor of the company, director of the company and any manager or trustee of any pension fund established for the benefit of employees of the company. Any of these people may object to the Registrar.

The Registrar will publish notice of the application in *The Gazette*. This will invite any person with valid objections to the striking-off to show cause why it should not happen. If no objections are made within three months of publication she may strike the company off. She will put a further notice in *The Gazette* to say that it has been done.

494 What are the possible pitfalls of a voluntary striking-off?

Any assets of the company pass to the Crown. You may wish Her Majesty to be the beneficiary but probably you do not, so you should ensure that the company's sole asset is ten pounds in the bank, which will be used to pay the fee for lodging form 652a with the Registrar. It is permitted to pay a dividend in order to reduce the assets to ten pounds and this does not count as carrying on business in the preceding three months. You will get into difficulties if the company is not solvent so be careful about this. There may also be problems if there are contingent liabilities. These could, for example, include a possible future action for alleged wrongful dismissal by a former employee.

495 My company has been the subject of a voluntary striking-off. Could it be restored to the register?

A person who should have been notified of the striking-off application may apply within 20 years to have the company's name restored to the register. The court may order this to be done if it considers that one of the following applies:

- The applicant was not given a copy of the application.

- The application involved a breach of duty under sections 652B(1) or 652B(3) of the Act.

- It is just to do so.

At the instigation of the registrar

496 Can a company be struck-off without the knowledge of the members or directors?

Yes, it can. The Registrar may strike-off a company that she believes is not in business or operation. She usually forms this opinion because the company does not submit accounts, an annual return or other documents, and because it ignores communications from her. It is often done because a company moves away from its registered office and neglects to inform Companies House on form 287, with the result that communications from the Registrar are not received.

497 What steps does the Registrar take before deciding to strike-off a company?

The steps to a striking-off at the instigation of the Registrar are as follows:

1. The Registrar will write to the company at its last notified registered office. This letter will enquire if the company is still in business or operation. If no response is received or documents filed, the Registrar will send a second letter by registered post. She will also write to each director at their last notified residential addresses.

2.   If no response is received, the Registrar will publish a notice in the *London Gazette* or *Edinburgh Gazette* giving notice of her intention to strike-off the company.

3.   The Registrar will place a copy of this notice on the company's file at Companies House. This warns any enquirer of her intention.

4.   The Registrar will consider any representations that may be received. These may be from the company, its officers, creditors or anyone at all.

5.   Not less than three months after placing the notice on the company's file at Companies House, the Registrar may strike-off the company.

498 I am a director of a company that has just been struck-off by the Registrar. Am I right to be angry?

The Registrar could have made a mistake but it is not likely. So no you should not be angry. Apologetic would be more appropriate. You presumably missed sending in at least one annual return and ignored at least one reminder. You presumably missed sending in at least one set of accounts and ignored progressive notifications of civil penalties. You also ignored two specific warnings to the company from the Registrar and a warning sent to your last notified residential address. Very probably you did not receive these reminders, notices and warnings to the company because you have moved away from your registered office, but that is not the Registrar's fault. You can hardly blame her for forming the opinion that the company is no longer in business or operation.

499 I am (or was) a director of a company that was struck-off even though it is still trading. What should I do?

The directors should apply to have the company restored to the register. This involves an application to the court and legal advice may well be necessary. All outstanding documents must be filed and all fines and penalties must be paid.

500 **During what period may an application be made to have a company restored to the register that was struck-off at the instigation of the Registrar?**

20 years.

501 **My company has been struck-off. Are officers of the company released from their liabilities?**

No.

Index

Index

The references in this index are to question numbers, not to page numbers.

board of directors

C

Combined Code

Companies House

D

Debentures

directors

E

F

G

N

O

P

Q

R

S

U

W

Update contact form

It is intended to regularly update this book and if you wish to be advised of new editions please fill in the following form and return to:

Thorogood Publishing Ltd
10-12 Rivington Street
London
EC2A 3DU

☐ **YES! Please notify me of any updates to *501 Questions for Company Directors and Company Secretaries* by Roger Mason as they become available.**

Name: _____

Job title: _____

Address: _____

_____

_____

_____

Telephone: _____

Email: _____

Fax: _____

Alternatively contact Thorogood Customer Services:
tel: 020 7749 4748, fax: 020 7729 6110 or email: info@thorogood.ws

Other titles from Thorogood

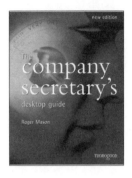

THE COMPANY SECRETARY'S DESKTOP GUIDE

Roger Mason
£16.99 paperback
Published April 2004

Written in a clear, jargon-free style, this is a comprehensive guide to the complex legislation and procedures governing all aspects of the company secretary's work. The Company Secretary's role becomes more demanding with every change to the law and practice. The author's considerable experience as both Company Secretary and lecturer and author has ensured a manual that is expert, practical and easy to access.

THE CREDIT CONTROLLER'S DESKTOP GUIDE
Proven procedures and techniques for getting paid on time and preserving cash

Roger Mason
£16.99 paperback
Published September 2004

Clear and jargon-free, this is an expert and practical guide to the techniques of effective credit control. This book takes account of all the recent changes to the law and practice, including: winding up, bankruptcy, receivership and administration, following implementation of The Enterprise Act 2002; statutory interest; obtaining judgment for unpaid debts; the abolition of Crown Preference and the effect on ordinary creditors; new rules concerning the recovery of VAT when there is a bad debt; what is available from Companies House; the latest thinking on retention of title clauses in conditions of sale.

COMPANY DIRECTOR'S DESKTOP GUIDE

David Martin
£16.99 paperback
Published June 2004

The role of the company director is fundamental to the success of any business, yet the tasks, responsibilities and liabilities that directors' face become more demanding with every change to the law.

Written in a clear, jargon-free style, this is a comprehensive guide to the complex legislation and procedures governing all aspects of the company director's role. The author's wide experience as a Director and Secretary of a plc and consultant and author provides a manual that is expert, practical and easy to access.

THE A-Z OF EMPLOYMENT PRACTICE

David Martin
£19.99 paperback, £42.00 hardback
Published November 2004

This book provides comprehensive, practical guidance on personnel law and practice at a time when employers are faced with a maze of legislation, obligations and potential penalties. It provides detailed and practical advice on what to do and how to do it.

The A to Z format ensures that sections appear under individual headings for instant ease of reference. The emphasis is not so much on the law as on its implications; the advice is expert, clear and practical, with a minimum of legal references. Checklists, procedures and examples are all given as well as warnings on specific pitfalls.